"This book is an amazing resource for teachers w
students develop both procedural fluency and c
Open Middle problems provide students with the opportunity to move beyond traditional procedural practice problems to explore mathematical relationships more deeply. In addition, Open Middle problems provide teachers with insights into what students really understand about the procedures they learned and important formative assessment data they can use to modify instruction. This book is a very practical guide to implementing a new class of tasks that have the potential to improve student learning!" **—DR. MARGARET (PEG) SMITH**

"Do you ever wish you could get a glimpse into a designer's mind for how they implement their innovation? Robert Kaplinsky's *Open Middle Math* gives educators an inside look into how Open Middle problems are designed to assist students to engage in, learn from, and persevere in productive struggle. Robert has always been willing to share his learning progress, struggles, and mistakes openly. Through his humility, he encourages readers to remember the joy that comes with productively struggling with a mathematics problem, and that we often learn more from the journey of solving than arriving at a solution. The mathematics education community will simply devour this delicious book."

—LAUREN BAUCOM

"Robert offers teachers strategies for adding openness and richness to problems that are at first closed and meager. So take heart, teachers! The interest and learning of your students aren't dictated by the problems in your textbook as you first find them, only by your imagination and design."

—DAN MEYER

"WARNING: Your students may not leave your mathematics classroom when the bell rings if you start using Open Middle tasks. In his book, Robert Kaplinsky gives math educators a roadmap to effectively implement *Open Middle Math* with tips, multiple examples at each secondary level, answers to the 'what ifs,' resources, and structures for creating your own tasks. . . . *Open Middle Math* is a quick read. A must read. A read with the potential for immediate transformation of the quality of discourse in your classroom."

—SARA VANDERWERF

"Reading *Open Middle Math: Problems That Unlock Student Thinking, Grades 6–12* is like having Robert as your thought partner as he strategically talks you through the rationale of, planning for, and implementation of Open Middle problems . . . [It] opened my eyes to the impact on students' conceptual understanding of secondary mathematics concepts. It helps the reader move pass a goal of just mathematical correctness to mathematical reasoning."

—JENISE SEXTON

"'Open Middle' problems are unique! Robert meets every 'what if' a math teacher can muster about implementing these tasks with his helpful, practical, play-by-play style. In reading and applying *Open Middle Math*, I feel like I have an experienced coach cheering me on!"

—CATHY YENCA

"Based on real classroom experience, Kaplinsky offers honest, practical, and actionable strategies to support you in transforming your classroom through Open Middle problems. Not only will your students experience mathematics in more authentic ways, but your teaching will be simultaneously energized as your classroom becomes a motivating space where students meet and enjoy the challenge of really doing mathematics."

—MATT LARSON

"*Open Middle Math* delves into transformative practices that are grounded around problems that promote creative problem solving. Robert Kaplinsky gives teachers a window into artful planning and pedagogy that provide us with the answer to the holy grail of all questions: 'What do students know and understand now?'"

—ALEXANDRA MARTINEZ

"If you are seeking to challenge your students' thinking and build their conceptual understanding, *Open Middle Math: Problems That Unlock Student Thinking, Grades 6–12* is a must-have resource. *Open Middle Math* will provide you with engaging, student-focused tasks, practical implementation strategies, and a wealth of support resources."

—DR. KRISTOPHER J. CHILDS

"I thought I knew everything about Open Middle problems until I read this book. Robert masterfully unpacks the complexity and beauty of these 'simple' problems and captures why they play an essential role in students' math experiences. Hearing his relatable experiences both as a teacher and learner will give you the confidence to hit the ground running. Buckle up and enjoy the ride!"

—DANIEL LUEVANOS

OPEN MIDDLE® MATH

Problems That Unlock Student Thinking, Grades 6–12

ROBERT KAPLINSKY

Stenhouse PUBLISHERS
PORTSMOUTH, NEW HAMPSHIRE

Library of Congress Cataloging-in-Publication Data
Names: Kaplinsky, Robert, 1978– author.
Title: Open middle math : problems that unlock student thinking, 6–12 / Robert Kaplinsky.
Description: Portsmouth, New Hampshire : Stenhouse Publishers, [2019] | Includes bibliographical references.
Identifiers: LCCN 2019016333 | ISBN 9781625311740 (pbk. : alk. paper)
Subjects: LCSH: Mathematics teachers—In-service training. | Mathematics teachers—Training of. | Middle school teachers—In-service training. | Middle school teachers—Training of. | Mathematics—Study and teaching (Middle school)
Classification: LCC QA10.5 .K37 2019 | DDC 510.71—dc23
LC record available at https://lccn.loc.gov/2019016333

Cover design by Tom Morgan
Interior design and typesetting by Shawn Girsberger

Manufactured in the United States of America

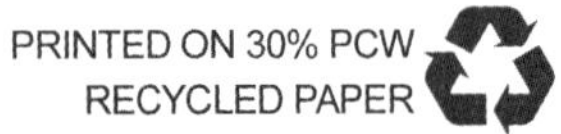

25 24 23 22 21 20 9 8 7 6 5 4 3 2

To my wife, Megan, and son, Owen.
I love you both.

CONTENTS

FOREWORD by Nanette Johnson

In the classroom, we have choices. When it appears that students don't understand what we're teaching them, we can explore their thoughts using questions, or we can express frustration about them not understanding the lesson being taught. After all, we were clear in our instructions when we delivered the lesson, so why don't they get it?

Our desire to uncover and explore students' thinking instead led Robert and me to start creating and collecting Open Middle problems. The problems reveal how deeply students understand what they're learning, often using fewer problems. They are designed to be more accessible, allowing educators to evaluate how students build conceptual understanding through their various attempts at solving a problem. Open Middle problems allow educators to peek into students' minds to see what mathematical understandings they have.

As an example, here's one of my favorite Open Middle problems:

"What is the least number of geometric markings needed to demonstrate that a quadrilateral is a square?"

How do you think a student might approach this problem? For example, a quadrilateral that used eight geometric markings (four markings for right angles and four markings for congruent sides) would be a square. So, we know 8 is a possible answer, but is it the *least* possible answer? Could a student demonstrate that a quadrilateral is a square in 7 markings or fewer? What exactly is a "geometric marking" anyway, and how might students define it? How might that intentional vagueness in the problem's wording push students' thinking further?

I vividly remember presenting this problem at a math educator conference. The discussion was exhilarating as teachers argued how their quadrilaterals used the least number of markings. In turn, other educators argued back, trying to convince them that their quadrilateral could be a non-square shape, like a parallelogram without right angles, or a kite.

In the midst of a collaborative discussion, I recall someone mentioning how the problem could be solved using "one marking if we just start with a circle . . ." This thoughtful and creative approach instantly set the room ablaze with excitement! I was personally amazed because, as the coauthor of this particular problem, not once had I ever considered using a circle as a geometric marking.

With traditional problems, students are told what steps to take and know when they have finished a problem. The bland, rote structure of traditional problems tends to limit flexibility and creativity and ultimately dampens the fervor of learning in most students. They check out, feel frustrated, or mindlessly follow the steps in their notes instead of thinking about and reflecting on their strategies.

In contrast, Open Middle problems often ask students to find strategically chosen types of answers such as the *least* or *greatest* solution or one that's *closest* to a certain number. This structure requires students to prove to themselves and others that they have truly found the best possible answer. Rather than putting down their pencils and saying, "I'm done," students continue to think, argue, and work. They develop the habit of making multiple attempts to solve the problem, each time wondering if they can come up with an even better solution than their last.

Let's face reality. We live in a digital age where the average person casually walks around with information at their fingertips from a powerful computer in their pocket. This is not what it was like when we were children. As a result, the kinds of skills and knowledge that were necessary and useful when we were growing up are not the same as what students need now.

Acknowledging this fact begs the question: are we really giving students the skills they need to be successful critical thinkers? If a smartphone can readily answer the problems we give them, are we giving them the right kinds of problem? Open Middle problems are designed to develop critical thinking, analytical reasoning, and problem solving, precisely because they are difficult to answer using a device, trick, or procedure.

The clear and powerful book that you are about to read will equip you with the skills, experience, and mindset required for educators to develop students into problem solvers. It provides you with what you need to compete against a culture that deems it completely acceptable, and even cool, to say, "I'm not a math person" or "I'm bad at math." It will help you answer the questions, "How do I know that my students really learned and can apply what they are learning?" and "Are students just imitating what I showed them, or do they deeply understand?" It will also guide you in your understanding of both why and how you can start implementing Open Middle problems right away.

I hope that *Open Middle Math* will excite you to explore what your students know and help them develop deeper mathematical understandings for what's ahead.

—*Nanette Johnson*

ACKNOWLEDGMENTS

Thank you to Nanette Johnson. You and I were fascinated by the potential of using math problems with open middles and incorporated them into our work as secondary math teacher specialists in Downey Unified School District. We've learned so much along the way by creating problems, implementing them with students, and sharing them with other educators. Everything that Open Middle has become would not have been possible without you.

Thank you to Dan Meyer, who has inspired and supported me in more ways than I can describe. Your generosity in sharing what you've learned has been transformative. Much of what I've created, from my problem-based lessons to the very idea of Open Middle itself, was influenced by you.

Thank you to Margaret (Peg) Smith and Mary Kay Stein for your amazing *5 Practices for Orchestrating Productive Mathematics Discussions* book. I had no idea how much better math discussions could be until I read your book. You'll see your influences in much of my work, including this book.

Thank you to everyone at Camino Nuevo Charter Academy, where I first began my teaching career, including Allison Whalen for helping me become a math teacher, Nancy Duran for molding me into a nurturing leader, Korinna Sánchez and Stephanie Siok Egan for being supportive, collaborative partners as we planned our lessons, and Lara Goldstone and Danielle Muller for your patient mentoring.

Thank you to everyone in Downey Unified School District, including all the educators I had the pleasure of collaborating with. Working at West Middle School felt like being with family. I learned so much from all of your experience. Your passion for students inspired me, and I cherish those memories. Thank you to Melissa Canham for helping me transition from working with students to working with fellow educators. You patiently guided me even though I naively thought I already knew it all. Thank you also to Glenda Martinez and Julie Yearsley for your insightful perspective and feedback. So much of the person I have grown to be is a result of the love and support from the Secondary Curriculum, Instruction, and Assessment team. Thank you to Denise Takano, Dalyn Miller-Geiser, Nanette Johnson, Charlotte Evensen, Karlin LaPorta, Paul Chun, Mark Schiavo, Gregg Stapp, and Nancy Valdez for telling me what I needed to hear and pushing me to become a better version of myself. Most of all, thank you to John Harris. Your faith and guidance brought out qualities I did not know I had. You are the kind of leader I aspire to be.

Thank you to Andrew Stadel, Christina Tondevold, Dan Finkel, Karim Ani, Graham Fletcher, Lybrya Kebreab, Fawn Nguyen, Ian Byrd, Kris Childs, Mark Goldstein, and Chase Orton. I deeply appreciate how you listen to me and give me support and advice. You are always there for me whenever I need you, and I'm fortunate to call you friends.

To Eric Milou, Matt Larson, Tim Kanold, and Steve Leinwand, thank you for mentoring me by sharing your experience and advice. Your generosity is what I think of when I try to help others.

Thanks to my writing buddy, Chris Luzniak. We finally finished our books, and I can't wait to read yours.

Thank you to everyone who has contributed to the Open Middle website, including the hundreds of educators who have submitted problems. Thank you to Nanette Johnson for cofounding Open Middle and being such an inclusive leader. Thank you to Bryan Anderson, who was the first to join our team and has spent hundreds of hours growing the site. Thank you to Dan Luevanos and Zack Miller, who came on next and contributed their knowledge and experience to the team. Thank you to Blanca Pacheco for translating the Open Middle worksheet to Spanish and to Jules Bonin-Ducharme for translating it to French. Thanks also to our growing team of volunteers, including Ashley Powell, Blanca Pacheco, Cecilia Calvo Pesce, Christa Amezcua,

Dan Shuster, Daniel Rocha, Debbie Vitale, Devin Rossiter, Diane Rodriguez, Dominique Bodin, Emma McCrea, Inés Ham, John Ulbright, Jules Bonin-Ducharme, Katie Bond, Keely Hulme, Kjersti Oliver, Kristine Cunningham, Laura Beth Place, Laura Wagenman, Marc Garneau, Mathías López, Molly Rawding, Owen Kaplinsky, Scott Hampton, TJ Luttrell, and Zach Berkowitz.

Thank you to DeLaina Ellis, Farica Erwin, Marguerite Spriggs, Pat Walter, and Wendy Kozina for sharing your experiences with Open Middle problems on social media and for allowing me to incorporate them into this book.

Thank you to the many amazing Southern California math teacher organizations, including the California Math Council (CMC), Orange County Math Council (OCMC), Greater San Diego Math Council (GSDMC), Greater Los Angeles Math Council (GLAMC), and the Southern California Math Teacher Specialist Network. So much of the outstanding work coming from Southern California exists because you tirelessly volunteer your time to create spaces for educators to collaborate. Personally, I am very grateful for all the opportunities you have given me. Without the work you put in to make incredible math conferences, I wouldn't have had opportunities to share and refine my ideas.

Thank you to all the national and international math educator communities, including the Benjamin Banneker Association (BBA), the National Council of Supervisors of Mathematics (NCSM), the National Council of Teachers of Mathematics (NCTM), TODOS, and of course the Math Twitter Blog-o-Sphere (#MTBoS). Whether in person or digitally, you've created countless opportunities for mathematics educators to share ideas. The group is always smarter than the smartest person in the group, and the interactions we've had have challenged and inspired me to improve my thinking more than I ever could have done on my own.

Thank you to the students who shared their thinking and work for this book. Teachers will really value seeing how you thought about the math problems you worked on.

Thank you to Lauren Baucom for reading through the entire book, tightening up my language, calling out unclear phrasing, double checking every math problem, and extending my thinking when there were other areas I could highlight. I really appreciate the knowledge and enthusiasm you generously shared.

To my editor, Tracy Zager, thank you for helping me find clearer ways to share my thinking and write a book I am proud of. You patiently guided me through this process, and your suggestions helped me see what was missing and were postdictably brilliant. I'm so fortunate to have had the opportunity to collaborate with you.

Big thanks to the entire Stenhouse production team including Jay Kilburn, Lynne Costa, and Shannon St. Peter as well as the copyeditor, proofreader, designer, and everyone else. I greatly appreciate how you navigated me through this process, designed a beautiful cover and interior, caught mistakes, and took care of all the little details that I only later figured out. Thanks also to Dan Tobin, president of Stenhouse, for being an accessible and creative thought partner for my random ideas.

Finally, thank you to my wife, Megan, and son, Owen. Megan, I appreciate how you take care of us and help me become a better version of myself. You're my best friend and the person I trust most to always have my back. I'm so grateful for the memories we've shared and look forward to all our adventures ahead. Owen, I am so proud of you. It's amazing to see you grow and learn, whether it's mathematics, bike riding, singing, acting, dancing, reading, ping pong, or board games. Thanks for being such a big supporter of everything I do (except my dad jokes). I love you so much.

INTRODUCTION
WHAT DOES AN OPEN MIDDLE CLASSROOM LOOK LIKE?

The bell rings and lunch ends. Sweaty students gather outside your classroom and slowly shuffle in, finding their seats. As the chatting softens and class begins, they look at you and the math problem you've written on the board. You're trying something new today and are cautiously optimistic about how this unfamiliar experience will be received. The problem looks different from what they're used to, and they wait for you to explain what to do.

As you describe the problem, you hear the groans and whispered resistance. Too many of your students believe that math is something where the teacher tells them what to do and then they repeat those steps dozens of times. This problem doesn't follow that pattern, and they're not sure what to make of it. Once you're done explaining the instructions, students begin working on the problem. They don't solve it on their first attempt, and the lesson begins to feel like many others you've taught. It's what happens next, though, that surprises you. Strangely, many of the students who often give up instead start trying the problem again. The familiar clink of pencils dropping onto the table as students check out is much fainter than usual. Slowly you start to notice a different energy taking over the room. Kids seem to be on a quest to figure out the answer.

Many students begin placing themselves in self-imposed friendly competitions against each other, struggling to see if they can improve upon their previous work. Those you frequently find daydreaming are actually excited to figure out how to get the best answer. Students who have felt comfortable with years of following the steps in their notes are unsure of what to make of the experience and have not fully bought in, but you're optimistic that they're on a path toward making sense of mathematics instead of just getting the answer. All you can see from students who normally finish assignments quickly and complain about being bored is the back of their heads and their furiously moving hands. Kids start chatting, going back and forth. Initially it sounds like they might be off task, but you realize that they're talking about the problem, whose answer is better, and how they got it. In fact, they're sharing math discoveries with each other like they're the first people to realize them, even though you've been telling them those same things for weeks.

Minutes fly by, and the time you'd normally spend keeping kids on task is spent guiding students who need help and facilitating powerful classroom conversations around problem-solving strategies. Students still have plenty of misconceptions, but you see them more easily than you ever have before, and they give you a clearer picture as to how you'll want to adjust future instruction.

Eventually the bell rings, but almost no one leaves. Instead, they beg you for a little more time to work on the problem. It feels like you're being pranked, because this can't possibly be happening. You remind them that they'll be late to their next class and have to leave. There's more groaning and whispered resistance, but this time it's for an entirely different reason. Slowly they get up, telling you that they loved this problem and hope to do another one tomorrow.

Some students are in fact late to their next class, and you get a call from their teacher to verify the outlandish excuse they gave. They said that the reason they were late was because they were working on a math problem in your class and didn't want to stop. Laughing to yourself, you confirm their reason and explain that it won't happen again. The other teacher hangs up in disbelief, and you stand there feeling the same way. You had hoped this was possible, but it wasn't until you saw it happen that you were able to believe it.

This story is not fantasy. Countless teachers have shared similar experiences about how their students responded to the problems and strategies you'll read about in this book. For example, Marguerite Spriggs, a geometry teacher from Long Island, New York, wrote,

> My first time trying an Open Middle problem with my students today. Wasn't sure how it would go or if they'd solve it. After a few minutes going at it (and coming up with more than one solution) they asked, "Can we do another one?" "That was fun—we should do it more!"

Fifth-grade teacher DeLaina Ellis from Kansas City, Missouri, wrote,

> It was an Open Middle showdown in 5th grade! They could NOT stop! One student even asked me for his paper during recess so he could try to get even closer!

Eighth-grade teacher Pat Walter added,

> Best thing I heard today while my students were doing their Open Middle bell ringer: "Go away, Mr. Walter! We don't need you. We're going to figure this out."

We love when moments like these happen, but they don't have to be random. With the right problems and planning, we can create moments like these consistently so that students see mathematics in an entirely different light.

To be clear, these changes rarely happen overnight. Many of our students think mathematics is about following the steps we give them, robotically computing answers. Shifting students' mindsets away from that reality won't be easy, but it will be worth it. Students who typically succeed in traditional math classes may feel uncomfortable and question why we're not just giving them the formula to solve the problem. It will take time for them to adjust to our new expectations. On the other hand, students who've typically checked out might become engaged thought leaders. These problems and the strategies I'll share for implementing them are not magic pills, but over time, you'll notice a huge shift in both your students' engagement and their mathematical thinking.

I wish I had figured these strategies out earlier in my career because when I began teaching, I taught my students much like I was taught. I showed them how to do a new skill and then gave them worksheets (often those ones where each problem gives a letter to answer a riddle) or dozens of problems from the textbook. Students sat in class, working on math like robots, waiting for the bell to ring. They were getting correct answers, yet they didn't seem to understand what they were doing. Somewhere in the back of my mind, I knew that these experiences didn't meet their needs well, but I didn't know what else I could do.

I was discouraged and overwhelmed because I was simultaneously flooded with strategies and resources I found online or were provided by my school, yet unable to find the ones that would actually meet my students' needs. I didn't know whether I had already been given what I needed, if it was out there if I looked long enough, or if it didn't even exist! I felt like I could do more, but I didn't feel like I had a path forward that I was comfortable with. I wanted to do better for my students, but I didn't know how to make it happen.

It took another ten years of mistakes and experimentation, but I eventually figured out practical and intuitive strategies we can use to meet our students' needs. In this book, we'll discuss those strategies as well as resources that we can use to support and challenge all of our students. When I've used them with other teachers through my trainings and website, they too found that they were game changers. The teachers talked about being excited and optimistic because they knew what they wanted to do, how they were going to do it, and why it was so important. They described students who were excited to do math and begged for more if they didn't offer these problems often enough. They even talked about becoming the teachers that parents requested for their children. So, my hope for writing this book is to share these strategies so that everyone could learn about them. While I'll share successes, I'll also be very up-front about the many challenges and mistakes I've made, as they're a natural part of every person's journey.

In Chapter One, called "How Will These Problems Help Me?" I'll begin with a thought experiment that helped me understand how I was able to pass my math classes as a student yet feel like a fake who could answer questions without really understanding what I was doing. You may find my story startlingly similar to your own experiences with learning mathematics and how some students score well on standardized assessments yet remain unprepared for their future math courses.

In Chapter Two, we'll talk about how we can stop this disconnect from happening. We'll explore Open Middle problems that will help us detect student misconceptions and strengthen their conceptual understanding. I'll share sets of three problems at all secondary grade levels, from sixth grade through calculus, and break them down so you can see how these problems apply to what you teach. You'll solve math problems that require increasing levels of thinking so you can experience the differences firsthand. This essential work will set us up for Chapters Three and Four, where we will dive in to how to use these problems with your students.

We'll begin the discussion about implementation in Chapter Three, where we'll talk about what we need to do before we use a problem with students. This preparation includes considering how we'll help students feel comfortable with solving a new type of problem in which the steps are not well defined, how we'll decide which problems to use with students, and how we'll use our planning time to ensure that our lesson both minimizes anxiety and leads to powerful experiences.

In Chapter Four, we'll build upon the preparation we did in Chapter Three as we talk about actually using a problem with students. We'll begin by examining how to get students started on Open Middle problems and include real-life drama, like what to do if students don't solve the problem using the method we had hoped they would and what to do if students solve the problem using a method we don't understand. We'll also discuss how to tell when productive struggle becomes unproductive struggle as well as how to help students get unstuck when they want to give up. Thinking about these sorts of issues will help us learn how to facilitate powerful classroom conversations.

In Chapter Five, I'll show you how to get more problems for your students, including where you can download hundreds of already made Open Middle problems. We'll also work through a three-step process for making your own problems or modifying existing ones. Finally, in Chapter Six, I'll encourage you to get started and help you consider your next steps for how to proceed.

Each chapter ends with a set of reflection questions because I've found that pausing and thinking about what I've read helps me better understand it. I hope these questions will be helpful for you to think about on your own, with in-person or online colleagues, or as part of a book study or class.

Here's what I hope comes next:

1. Read this book for actionable ideas you can use to challenge students, facilitate powerful classroom conversations, and learn more about students' misconceptions.

2. Share what you learn in-person with other educators and on social media. Be sure to tag me (@robertkaplinsky) and use the #OpenMiddleBook hashtag.

3. Keep coming back to this book when you have a question or need a refresher by looking at the table of contents to find the section that addresses your concerns.

Also, if you'd like to download digital copies of the resources I share in this book so you can have them next to you as you read, either text the code OMBOOK to 44222, scan the QR code, or go to robertkaplinsky.com/ombook and enter your information there. After you enter your information, the resources will be automatically emailed to you.

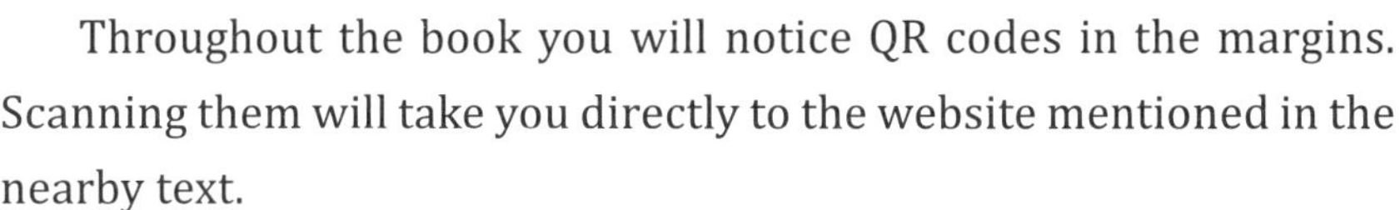

Throughout the book you will notice QR codes in the margins. Scanning them will take you directly to the website mentioned in the nearby text.

No teacher likes it when their students have hidden misconceptions they don't uncover until a big assessment or when their class has both students who find the classwork too easy and students who are completely lost. I've been there many times, and I've written this book to share everything I've learned about making these issues much less common. I hope these strategies help you along your journey as I know they've helped me along mine.

CHAPTER ONE
HOW WILL THESE PROBLEMS HELP ME?

Have you ever felt like your students understood what you taught them, only to find out later that you were mistaken? This has happened to me more times than I can count! What made this feel especially frustrating was that I didn't see these issues coming during the lessons. It really seemed like they understood what I was teaching them, and I rarely figured out that I was mistaken until after I saw the assessment results and was already teaching something else.

These experiences made me wonder why I didn't realize these issues earlier. After all, I was asking students questions and they were getting them right. So how was it possible they didn't understand? What was I doing wrong? I didn't feel like I understood where the breakdown was happening until I came across a thought experiment from philosopher John Searle called the Chinese Room.

In this thought experiment, imagine a man who does not speak Chinese, sitting in a room. He has been given a box of Chinese characters as well as a book that lists both the characters he might receive from someone outside the room and what characters he should send back in return. Then, a woman who speaks Chinese fluently comes up to the room, writes a few Chinese characters on a piece of paper, and slips the paper under the door. The man inside picks it up, looks in the book to see what characters he should send back, picks the appropriate Chinese characters from the box, and slides the response under the door to the woman outside.

Let's consider each person's perspective. The woman outside the room slipped a paper to the man that said, "Do you speak Chinese?"

and received the response "Yes, fluently." So, from her perspective, the man inside the room speaks Chinese. However, from the perspective of the man inside the room, he was just following a procedure he'd been given. He probably has no idea what message he received or what message he sent back. He would likely say that he does not speak Chinese.

When I first heard this thought experiment, my immediate realization was, "I'm the man inside the Chinese Room but with mathematics instead of Chinese!" I remember this phenomenon beginning in my eighth-grade algebra class. My teacher would give me a problem that I would solve using a formula I had written in my notes. I didn't really understand what the problem was asking or what the formula did, but I could figure out what information I was supposed to give back in return and turned in the correct answer to my teacher.

Let's consider each person's perspective. The teacher gave me a problem to solve and received a correct answer back. So, from her perspective, I understood what she was teaching me and demonstrated it by solving the problem. However, from my perspective, I was just plugging numbers into a formula from my notes. I did not really understand what information I received or what I gave back. The only thing I was sure of was that I felt like a fake who did not understand algebra or, later, the mathematics I would do in high school and college.

Unfortunately, it's been my experience that many educators can relate to this story, either as the person inside the Chinese Room, the one outside of it, or both. As educators, it's scary to think that we may not have the tools we need to determine whether our students really understand what we teach them. After all, we would hope that assessment questions like those on standardized tests would be able to measure true understanding. Maybe not.

One impactful moment in my career happened soon after I transitioned from being a middle school mathematics teacher to a mathematics teacher specialist in Downey Unified School District. I was teaching a lesson at one of our high schools, and many of my former students were in this class. The lesson I was teaching that day was on point-slope form, and I was eager to see what they knew. To my astonishment, the students told me that they had never learned about slope. We've all heard something like that before, and maybe sometimes it's true, but this time it was baloney because *I* was the teacher who had taught it to most of them in seventh grade!

I was stunned because the vast majority of these students had earned "advanced" or "proficient" (one of the two highest levels) on our state standardized test. How was it possible that students could earn such high scores yet not be able to build upon what they knew? They didn't even have a memory of learning about it! I reflected on this for quite some time, and what I finally came to realize was that *I* was the problem.

I felt embarrassed because, while I thought these kids were proficient or advanced, I was wrong. Many students were really at much lower proficiency levels, but I didn't have a clue. Looking back, I realized that when they were in my classroom, I had asked them superficial questions about slope. I came to understand that when I asked students superficial questions, I got superficial information back about what they knew. I clearly had students with huge gaps in their understanding, but I couldn't identify who they were or where they had misconceptions.

I CAME TO UNDERSTAND THAT WHEN I ASKED STUDENTS SUPERFICIAL QUESTIONS, I GOT SUPERFICIAL INFORMATION BACK ABOUT WHAT THEY KNEW.

In retrospect, I realize that this made me feel especially awful because I was repeating the pattern and putting my own math students inside the Chinese Room. I was slipping problems under the door for students to solve and they were returning correct answers that made me think that they understood what I was teaching them. I realized that I needed to find a more reliable way of determining whether students authentically understood what they were learning instead of just repeating the steps in their notes. I wished that I had something like X-ray vision glasses, which could let me look into their brains and see their mathematical misconceptions.

It was a challenging emotion to process, but I was motivated to find a reliable way to determine where my students struggled and help them develop deeper mathematical understandings. I needed to break my students out of the Chinese Room, and I realized that my overemphasis on students' answers instead of their mathematical thinking was part of the problem.

I needed a different approach that would value their journey toward the solution as much as the solution itself. I wanted kids debating about the best way to solve the problem rather than simply racing to get correct answers. I wanted them to use more strategic thinking instead of mindlessly using the formula I had just given them. Most of all, I wanted to know when my students had misconceptions so I could do something about them.

After learning from experts like Norman Webb and Dan Meyer, and then much experimentation and collaboration with my colleague Nanette Johnson and others (more on this in Chapter Two), I figured out how to make and facilitate a kind of problem that would do just what I was looking for. These problems, called Open Middle problems, help me identify students' misunderstandings, even when the kids don't realize they have any. They motivate both students who struggle as well as those looking for more challenge, all while having kids engaged and craving more mathematics. You can easily substitute the problems for what you're already doing with your students instead of adding yet another item to a jam-packed school year to-do list.

To be sure, using Open Middle problems does not eliminate student misconceptions entirely. However, since using them, I now see student misconceptions more clearly and can use them as talking points to strengthen mathematical understandings during the lesson instead of simply lamenting missed opportunities afterward. I've also used them to make more meaningful assessments that provide me with richer information using fewer questions. This type of assessment gives me more accurate results and allows me to spend more time on instruction and less on testing.

I hope you're excited to see how you could use these problems to help your students. So, let's explore Open Middle problems to see how they're different from some of the other problems we've used.

REFLECTION QUESTIONS

Here are some questions for you to reflect on by yourself, with your colleagues, or on social media using the #OpenMiddleBook hashtag.

- What was a time when you felt like your students understood what you taught them, only to find out later that you were mistaken?
- How is it possible that students could correctly answer questions on standardized tests yet not fully understand what they had learned?
- How would having a clearer picture of students' understandings and misconceptions affect how we taught them?

CHAPTER TWO
HOW ARE OPEN MIDDLE PROBLEMS DIFFERENT?

When I first started playing around with Open Middle problems, I knew that they looked different and made me think a little more, but I didn't understand what made them special. It wasn't until I started using multiple problems on the same mathematical concept that I was able to see how important these differences were.

To show you what I mean, I want to walk you through three problems on solving one-step equations so we can talk about what makes them different from one another. First, we'll talk about a traditional problem. I'm sure you can imagine finding dozens of problems that are similar to it in any middle school mathematics textbook. Find the answer and then read on.

Problem 1

Solve for *x*.

$$21 + x = 70$$

When solving this problem, you likely found that $x = 49$ by either subtracting 21 from both sides of the equals sign or by asking yourself, "Twenty-one plus what number equals seventy?" I wondered how challenging it would be for students, so I used social media to ask teachers to try this problem with their students and let me know what percentage answered it correctly. Out of the 1,120 sixth and seventh graders who attempted the problem, about 92 percent (1,030 students) correctly determined that $x = 49$.

It probably doesn't come as a surprise to you that such a large percentage of students solved it correctly. What I wondered, though, was whether asking students this one question (or a whole worksheet of this type of question) was enough to determine how deeply they understood solving one-step equations.

To figure this out, I created another problem on the same topic and standard. Spend some time solving this second problem, and then estimate the percentage of sixth- and seventh-grade students that would be able to solve it:

Problem 2

> Using the digits 1 to 9 at most one time each, place a digit in each box to create two equations: one where x has a positive value and one where x has a negative value. You may reuse all the digits for each equation.
>
> $\square\square + x = \square\square$

This problem is more challenging than the first one. The missing digits make it impossible to jump straight into computation. Most people begin the problem by randomly placing a digit in each box to see what happens. For example, the equation $12 + x = 34$ would result in x having a positive value of 22. But now a little more thinking comes from the process of trying to find the negative value. How do you arrange the digits to make x's value negative?

One possibility is to guess and check, playing around with the digits until x has a negative value. That would eventually work but could take a while. Alternatively, you might think about it conceptually. If the number being added to x is greater than the sum, x must be negative.

For example, in the equation $34 + x = 12$, there is nothing positive that you could add to 34 to get 12. So, you can just swap the 12 and 34 in the first equation and get $x = -22$.

After a combination of guessing and checking, noticing patterns, and using conceptual understanding, people start to generalize their experiences. While there are many potential answers, x has a positive value when the number being added to x is less than the sum. It has a negative value when the number being added to x is greater than the sum.

I don't know about you, but for me, the second problem made me think differently than anything I remember doing when I was a student or used when I was a new teacher. Sure, I incorporated problems that had boxes to fill with digits, but the thinking needed to complete them was closer to what we experienced with a traditional worksheet. I didn't have to stop and think conceptually about how the digits I chose affected the results.

I asked those same teachers to also try Problem 2 with their students, and only about 51 percent (571 students) of the 1,120 students correctly solved it! This is a huge difference from Problem 1, so let's stop and think about what this means.

Problem 1 showed us that about 92 percent of the students could correctly solve a one-step equation problem while Problem 2 showed us that a much lower 51 percent of the students could correctly solve a different one-step equation problem. If you agree that a student who deeply understands one-step equations should be able to solve both problems, then this implies that about 41 percent of the students didn't really know what they were doing. They might have appeared to understand the concept if teachers only gave them Problem 1, but in reality, they had much weaker understandings that weren't uncovered until they encountered Problem 2. What's scary about this is that I used to *only* use problems like Problem 1, so hundreds of my students may not have understood what I was teaching them . . . and I was clueless about it.

Problem 2 is our first example of how an Open Middle problem can give us X-ray vision because it helped us identify students' misunderstandings—even if they didn't realize they had any—and helped reveal what students actually knew. I believe that if we use problems only like the first one, there would be a good chance that many of our students would look like they were proficient, even if there were some hidden misconceptions. What I wondered, though, was whether the second problem was enough to measure deep understanding. While it helped uncover some misconceptions, could there have been even more gaps that it didn't uncover?

I decided to use a third problem to see what else I could learn about students' (mis)understandings of one-step equations. Take some time to solve Problem 3 and then estimate the percentage of students that would be able to correctly answer the problem:

Problem 3

> Using the digits 1 to 9 at most one time each, place a digit in each box to create an equation where *x* has the greatest possible value.
>
> $\square\square + x = \square\square$

This problem requires more concentration and brainpower to solve than Problems 1 and 2. It builds upon the second problem, making you think very specifically about how placing the missing digits affects *x*'s value. If students don't use conceptual understanding, they'll have to guess and check for a while before they find the correct answer. However, if they do use conceptual understanding, they may realize that when the number being added to *x* has a very small value and the sum's value is very large, then x will need to have a large value to make up the difference. As a result, $12 + x = 98$ will give x the greatest possible value because you can't make a two-digit number with a lesser value than 12 or a greater value than 98.

In reflecting on Problem 3, there are similar points I want you to consider. Again, the standard and topic are the same as with Problems 1 and 2. However, while guessing and checking may have worked well enough for the first and second problems, it's painfully inefficient for this third problem. If students don't conceptually understand how one-step equations work, they could be guessing and checking for quite a long time. To solve the problem efficiently, they must develop and use conceptual understanding by noticing patterns in how x's value changes.

When teachers gave Problem 3 to the same 1,120 students, only about 37 percent (414 students) of them could solve it correctly! Think about what these results imply if our students are similar to the surveyed students and we assume that students who solved Problems 2 and 3 also solved Problem 1. If we used only Problem 1, we would be content to know that about 92 percent of our students understood how to solve one-step equations and could move on to the next topic. If we also used Problem 2, we would realize that an intervention was needed because nearly half of our students had weak understandings. If we used Problem 3 as well, we would see that about 63 percent of students could not solve it, and we might even want to reconsider how we taught one-step equations! It's unsettling to realize how dramatically different we would feel about what students knew, based on the problem we chose to use.

I can't emphasize this point enough. If we just use problems like Problem 1 and not Open Middle problems like Problems 2 and 3, then there will likely be many students who will appear to understand what we're teaching them but will really have critical hidden misconceptions. In this particular case, 616 students (55 percent of the 1,120 students) had mathematical misunderstandings we would not have noticed if we had just used Problem 1. They were uncovered only by using Problems 2 and 3. Unfortunately, I've found that students have hidden misconceptions much more frequently than I initially realized. Almost every time I think my students fully understand what I'm teaching them, I find out that there are misconceptions I've been unaware of until I use an Open Middle problem.

ALMOST EVERY TIME I THINK MY STUDENTS FULLY UNDERSTAND WHAT I'M TEACHING THEM, I FIND OUT THAT THERE ARE MISCONCEPTIONS I'VE BEEN UNAWARE OF UNTIL I USE AN OPEN MIDDLE PROBLEM.

This is a big deal because for many years, standardized assessments have relied heavily on problems like Problem 1 to determine students' proficiency. As a result, many students (certainly including my own) may have been mistakenly labeled as mathematically proficient when in reality they were not. With the surveyed students, more than half of them fell into the false-positive gap. This gap is something we should seek to close if we want all students to make sense of mathematics.

If you're like me and you've primarily taught by using problems similar to Problem 1, then the potential of incorporating Open Middle problems like Problems 2 and 3 will make you both curious and concerned about how your students will do. It's not fun to realize that our students are not making sense of mathematics, but quickly getting actionable data will make fixing this issue easier.

So, let's continue our exploration of Open Middle problems by trying out problems more relevant to what you teach. There is no better way to understand what makes these problems different from one another than by experiencing them yourself. Once you've worked on a few of them, you'll have better perspective as to what makes them different from traditionally used problems.

Problems at Each Grade Level

This section does *not* have to be read straight through like a normal book. I've listed sets of secondary math problems covering topics from sixth grade through calculus. I want you to begin by picking a set of problems on a topic that interests you. For example, if you teach Algebra 1, you might begin with Algebra 1 problems, or you might choose the eighth-grade problems so that you can see what students might do before coming to your class.

Next, I want you to do all three problems from that set, in order, beginning with Problem 1, then Problem 2, and finally Problem 3. Taking the time to solve the problems yourself and doing them in order are very important. Do not move on or read anything else in this book until you've completed or spent significant time on all three problems in the set you chose. Once you're done with the set, read that set's reflection, where I break down and compare the three problems you just did. As you will have just completed the set, you'll have the experience and context necessary to appreciate the differences among the problems. I suggest you repeat this process with another set of Open Middle problems (so that you've done at least two sets), but feel free to try as many as you like.

While you're doing the problems, pay careful attention to how you feel. This might sound silly, but think about how your stress level changes as you progress from Problem 1 to Problem 2 to Problem 3. How much more mental effort does each problem in a set take? Does the additional challenge excite you or make you want to shut down? These experiences will give you great perspective because your students will experience similar emotions. You'll find it easier to empathize with and support students in their growth if you understand what they're going through. Every person who struggles values hearing that others have had similar experiences. Believe me, I still struggle when I try to solve many of these problems, and in this book, I'll share stories of times I found out that my "correct" answer was not really correct.

Remember that while you do not need to do the problems from every single grade level, you should complete the problems within each set in the order presented. While you can do as many sets as you like, completing two or three sets will give you sufficient experience for Chapter Three, where we talk about how to use Open Middle problems with your students. Once you've finished as many problem sets as you'd like to do, feel free to skip to page 48, where we'll reflect on what we learned.

SIXTH-GRADE EXAMPLE

DIVIDING FRACTIONS

Problem 1

Evaluate.

$$\frac{4}{9} \div \frac{3}{5}$$

Problem 2

Using the digits 1 to 9 at most one time each, place a digit in each box to make two different pairs of fractions that have a quotient of $\frac{2}{3}$.

$$\frac{\square}{\square} \div \frac{\square}{\square} = \frac{2}{3}$$

Problem 3

Using the digits 1 to 9 at most one time each, place a digit in each box to make two fractions that have a quotient that is as close to $\frac{4}{11}$ as possible.

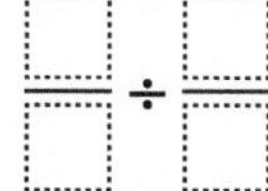

» Reflection

With Problem 1, students can solve it by using the traditional dividing fractions algorithm and don't necessarily have to make sense of what they are doing because they can just repeat the steps in their notes. They will often invert and multiply to change the problem to $\frac{4}{9} \cdot \frac{5}{3}$ and get an answer of $\frac{20}{27}$. Even if students correctly completed an entire worksheet of these problems, it would be hard to tell which students deeply understood what they were doing and which were robotically repeating the steps they were told to use.

With Problem 2, the first thing to notice is that students cannot immediately jump into calculations because there are no fractions for them to divide. To begin, they must choose which digits they want to use. Initially, they may randomly pick four digits and place them, but after a few rounds of that, they might realize that guessing and checking could take a long time. Instead, they must pause and use their conceptual understanding of how fraction division works to determine which numbers to pick.

For example, they may think about how the reciprocal of the fraction to the right of the division symbol will eventually be multiplied with the fraction to the left of the division symbol and think about choosing digits to form fractions that would simplify to $\frac{2}{3}$ when multiplied together. One example would be $\frac{4}{2} \div \frac{3}{1}$, which would become $\frac{4}{2} \cdot \frac{1}{3}$ and simplify to $\frac{2}{3}$. Alternatively, they could think of dividing the numerators and the denominators separately and choose digits to form $\frac{2}{9} \div \frac{1}{3}$. This is equivalent to $\frac{(2 \div 1)}{(9 \div 3)}$, which also equals $\frac{2}{3}$. I'm sure you can imagine students who could solve Problem 1 correctly but not Problem 2, so the X-ray vision that this Open Middle problem provides would give you an opportunity to both address students' misconceptions and have rich conversations about conceptual understanding of dividing fractions.

Problem 3 is so much harder than it first appears. It's important to note that it's not possible to get exactly $\frac{4}{11}$ because the denominator is a prime number. So, the question you might have asked yourself at some point was, "How do I know that my answer is the closest?" When I first solved the problem, I got $\frac{5}{7} \div \frac{2}{1}$. I knew that $\frac{5}{14}$ was relatively close to $\frac{4}{11}$, but I wasn't sure how to verify whether it was the closest quotient. Ultimately, after collaborating with other educators, we found that the most conclusive way to find the quotient that was closest to $\frac{4}{11}$ was to use software to try every possibility. We found that my answer (along with equivalents that also had a quotient of $\frac{5}{14}$, like $\frac{5}{7} \div \frac{4}{2}$, $\frac{5}{7} \div \frac{6}{3}$, and $\frac{5}{7} \div \frac{8}{4}$ as well as $\frac{2}{4} \div \frac{7}{5}$, $\frac{1}{2} \div \frac{7}{5}$, $\frac{3}{6} \div \frac{7}{5}$, $\frac{4}{8} \div \frac{7}{5}$) was indeed the closest to $\frac{4}{11}$.

What's important to realize about a problem like this is that the journey matters much more than the destination. Once students have had time to make several attempts, you can ask them to talk with their classmates to figure out who has the closest quotient. Kids will start chatting about what fractions they picked and how to best check whose quotient is closer. "Should we use common denominators? Unit fractions? A calculator?" In a quest to find the closest quotient, they might point out when other students have made a mistake or have an equivalent quotient. Some might think that they could still do better and keep looking for other possibilities.

At this point, you can walk around the room with X-ray vision, carefully listening to conversations that will give you rich information about what your students really know about dividing fractions and what misconceptions they still have. Open Middle problems like Problems 2 and 3 help students develop conceptual understanding and give you the formative data you need to intervene, as necessary. The experience also comes with the added benefit of significant embedded practice. In doing one of these Open Middle problems, students may wind up doing the equivalent of ten or fifteen problems like Problem 1.

Keep reading for more examples or go to page 48 to continue book.

SEVENTH-GRADE EXAMPLE
SOLVING TWO-STEP EQUATIONS

Problem 1

Solve for x.

$$2x + 3 = 9$$

Problem 2

Using the digits 1 to 9 at most one time each, place a digit in each box to create two equations: one where x has a positive value and one where x has a negative value. You may reuse all the digits for each equation.

$$\square x + \square = \square$$

Problem 3

Using the digits 1 to 9 at most one time each, place a digit in each box to create an equation where x has the greatest possible value.

$$\square x + \square = \square$$

Reflection

Problem 1 is typical of the two-step equations you see in textbooks and worksheets. While students may certainly struggle with a problem like this, correctly solving it does not guarantee that they fully understand it either. Students might guess and check, trying to plug in values for x until they find a value that makes $2x+3=9$ true. They might also think, "What number do I know that when doubled equals six?" so that $6+3=9$. Or they might perform operations like subtracting 3 from both sides to give them $2x=6$ and then dividing both sides by 2 (or switching back to guessing and checking). Eventually, you'd expect students to have correct answers for all their problems, but again, does that guarantee that they deeply understand how to solve two-step equations?

You may have noticed that Problem 2 is the two-step-equation version of the one-step equation problem we explored at the beginning of the chapter. The first thing to realize is that students cannot immediately jump into computations because there are no digits for them to perform operations on. To begin, they must choose which digits they want to use. Initially, they may randomly pick three digits and place them, but after a few rounds of that, they may realize that guessing and checking could take a long time. Now they must pause and use their conceptual understanding of two-step equations to determine which numbers to pick.

For example, if they initially choose 2, 1, and 5 as the digits to use and make $2x+1=5$, they will find that x's value is 2 and that they have the positive solution. Now they must stop and think about their options. They could continue to guess and check to find the negative value, but again that could take a while. Or they could use their conceptual understanding to figure out how the coefficients and constants affect x's value. This Open Middle problem would allow you to walk around the room, looking for students whose guessing and checking showed you that they needed your help.

Problem 3 builds upon Problem 2, but while guessing and checking might have worked for some students on Problem 2, it's much less likely to work now. Students may begin by trying to place the 9. They may initially put it as the coefficient but then later realize that this will make a lesser value because they will have to divide by 9 at some point. Next, they might put the 9 as the constant being added to the *x* term, but they'll eventually realize that this will be subtracted from what *x* equals and so that value will be lesser as well. Finally, they might try 9 as the sum and realize that this is the ideal place to put it. As for the coefficient and constant, they now know they should be lesser values, but which one should be a 1 and which should be a 2? Does it matter? How do they know? Think about the arguments and conversations you could have at this point. You could even put up $1x + 2 = 9$ and $2x + 1 = 9$ and have students argue about how they know which one would result in *x* having a greater value. Students may argue procedurally that $1x + 2 = 9$ results in $x = 7$ and that $2x + 1 = 9$ results in $x = 4$. Or they may argue conceptually that because they will have to divide by the coefficient, they want that digit to be as small as possible, as the constant will be subtracted. Again, Problem 3 is an Open Middle problem that provides X-ray vision because when students work on it, you can more clearly see their thinking and get a more detailed picture of what they know or don't know about two-step equations as well as gain insight about students' mathematical processes and practices.

Keep reading for more examples or go to page 48 to continue book.

EIGHTH-GRADE EXAMPLE
EVALUATING EXPONENTS

Problem 1

Evaluate.

3^4

Problem 2

Using the digits 1 to 9 at most one time each, place a digit in each box to make two true number sentences. You may reuse all the digits for each number sentence.

$\square^{\square} = 64$

Problem 3

Using the digits 1 to 9 at most one time each, place a digit in each box to make the greatest possible result.

$\square^{\square} = \square\square\square$

Reflection

While students might correctly solve Problem 1, they might also multiply 3 by 4 to get 12. So, while an incorrect answer would signal that there might be a misconception, a correct answer would not necessarily mean students had deep conceptual understanding.

With Problem 2, students will likely be drawn to 8^2 as their first number sentence. If the problem required only one number sentence, that might be the end of the exploration, but since it requires finding a second number sentence, it leads students to other possibilities. Students might initially think that there are no other ways to get 64 as they may be more familiar with perfect squares. Eventually they should find that 2^6 and 4^3 also equal 64.

Finally, Problem 3 will really test students' conceptual understanding. This problem is solvable by anyone with a calculator and plenty of time. However, students with conceptual understanding can greatly minimize the quantity of expressions they need to check. For example, students can eliminate exponents of 1 and 2 because they won't give three-digit results, no matter what digit is chosen for the base. They can also eliminate 9 as an exponent for most bases as 2^9 is a three-digit number and 3^9 is a five-digit number. Similarly, bases with values of 6, 7, 8, and 9 can be eliminated when used with a exponent of 4 or greater as 6^4 is a four-digit number, therefore 7^4, 8^4, and 9^4 are also not options as they would have even greater values.

It's also worth noting why there are three boxes for the digits in the result, because that was a choice I had to think about when creating the problem. If there were no boxes there, the problem would be much less interesting. Students would check to see whether the greatest possible result was 8^9 or 9^8 and be done. Similarly, having only one or two boxes would greatly limit the possibilities and make the problem less interesting as well. If there were four or more boxes, there would be so many possibilities to check that it would become a very frustrating problem. So, having three digits in the result seemed to be a good compromise between bringing out the thinking I was looking for without making students perform endless calculations.

When I first made this problem, I found two optimal answers: $9^3 = 729$ and $3^6 = 729$. It was months later before someone pointed out that $9^3 = 729$ was not a possible answer because I had used the 9 more than once. This process of revision is a common part of working with Open Middle problems and is both humbling and rewarding.

I want to point out that students' journey toward the answer is as important as whether they correctly answer the problem or not. Students who work on this problem but don't find the greatest possible result will likely develop more conceptual understanding and more procedural fluency with exponents than students who work on a worksheet of problems similar to Problem 1. Additionally, the information you gain about how your students think and work will likely be much richer.

Keep reading for more examples or go to page 48 to continue book.

ALGEBRA EXAMPLE

INTERPRETING KEY FEATURES OF QUADRATICS IN VERTEX FORM

Problem 1

Find the roots and maximum of the quadratic equation.

$$y=-2(x-3)^2+8$$

Problem 2

Using the digits 1 to 9 at most one time each, place a digit in each box to create two different quadratic equations that have a root at 4 and a maximum value of 4. You may reuse all the digits for each equation.

$$y=-\square(x-\square)^2+\square$$

Problem 3

Using the digits 1 to 9 at most one time each, place a digit in each box to create a quadratic equation with the greatest maximum value.

$$y=-\square(x-\square)^2+\square$$

Reflection

Problem 1 is fairly typical of what students working on quadratics in vertex form might be required to do. Students should know that the quadratic has a maximum value (and no minimum value) because a is negative. They might find the quadratic's vertex at (h, k) or $(3, 8)$, giving a maximum value of 8. They can then find the roots by setting $y = 0$ and determining that there are roots at $x = 1$ and $x = 5$. Alternatively, students might solve the equation by isolating x and undoing the operations, or they may think of a value that balances the equation to equal 0.

While you've likely had students who got problems like this wrong, does getting it right mean that students have deep understandings of quadratics in vertex form? For example, students might know that (h, k) is where the maximum or minimum occurs, but guess as to whether it's the x- or y-value they should focus on for the actual value. So, how do we ensure that students are not stuck in the Chinese Room (see Chapter One), plucking numbers from formulas and coming up with answers without understanding?

With Problem 2, the standard has not changed, yet the manner in which students approach the problem has. Students can no longer mindlessly use the formulas in their notes without thinking about the implications. They might begin by guessing and checking, randomly selecting digits for each box. If they never grow beyond that strategy, this problem will take quite a long time. Hopefully, students will eventually notice a pattern or use their conceptual understanding and realize that because the maximum value is 4, the box that represents k must be a 4. While this idea narrows down the possibilities, there are still 56 options that require checking.

If students use their conceptual understanding and approach the problem algebraically, they may realize that the quadratic will have a root at 4 when $x = 4$ and $y = 0$. If they simplify $0 = -a(4 - h)^2 + 4$, they will get $(4-h)=\frac{\pm 2}{\sqrt{a}}$. At this point, they might use their conceptual understanding to realize that *a*'s value must be a perfect square. Otherwise, *a* will be irrational, and it will be impossible to find an integer root. This insight narrows *a*'s values down to 1, 4, and 9. Because the digit 4 is already being used by *k*, *a* must be 1 or 9.

Now students can solve two different equations and check far fewer values: $(4-h)=\frac{\pm 2}{\sqrt{1}}$ and $(4-h)=\frac{\pm 2}{\sqrt{9}}$. This will yield four equations that have roots at 4:

1. $y=-1(x-2)^2+4$
2. $y=-1(x-6)^2+4$
3. $y=-9\left(x-3\frac{1}{3}\right)^2+4$
4. $y=-9\left(x-4\frac{2}{3}\right)^2+4$

As *h* has to be an integer value, students will be left with only two possible answers: $a=1$, $h=2$, and $k=4$ or $a=1$, $h=6$, and $k=4$.

Alternatively, students might approach this problem graphically. If they use a graphing program like Desmos, which has sliders (see Figure 2.1), then they can set $k=4$ and see how changing the values of *a* and *h* affect the quadratic's roots. They may similarly realize that some values of *a* do not produce roots with integer values and may gravitate to *a* being equal to 1 or 9. Ultimately, they should find the same equations of $y=-1(x-2)^2+4$ and $y=-1(x-6)^2+4$, which are the same graph, just translated horizontally.

If students have not grown beyond guess-and-check strategies and use no conceptual understanding, Problem 3 will be a nightmare for them. There are 504 possible combinations of digits, and it would take a while to figure out which ones resulted in the maximum value of all possibilities.

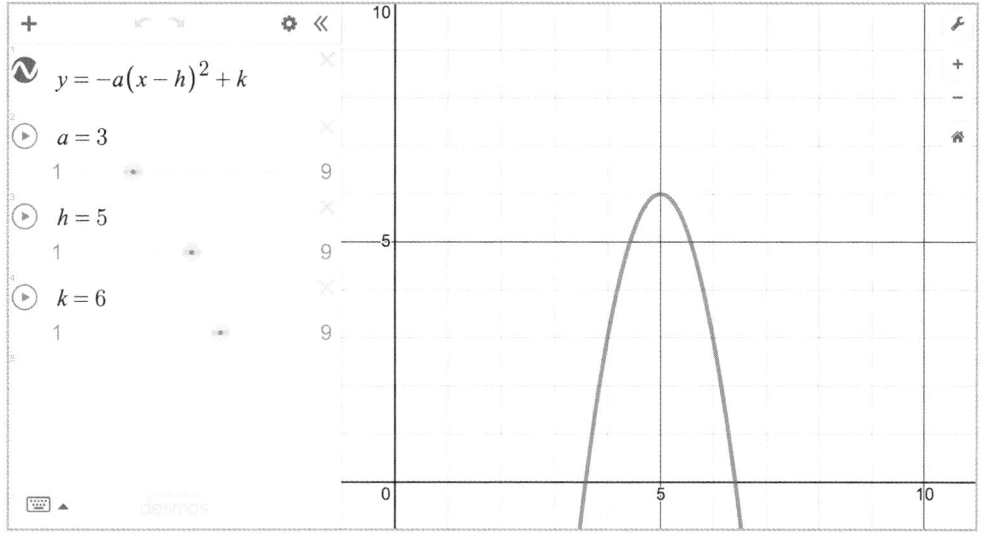

FIGURE 2.1

What is the greatest maximum value? *(Powered by Desmos)*

Like Problem 2, Problem 3 can also be approached algebraically, graphically, or using a combination of both. Fortunately, this problem lends itself toward students noticing patterns and building conceptual understanding. Students' first insight might be to notice that *k*'s value happens to be the same as the maximum value. Then they might realize that *k*'s value must be 9 because that is the greatest possible value with the available digits. Next, students might try different digits for *a* and *h* to see how they affect the quadratic's maximum value. Ultimately, students should realize that regardless of the digits chosen for *a* and *h*, the maximum value remains the same! Again, without developing conceptual understanding, students would be stuck with a very long process of guessing and checking, so the X-ray vision this Open Middle problem will give you will really help you determine what students know.

Keep reading for more examples or go to page 48 to continue book.

GEOMETRY EXAMPLE
FINDING THE MIDPOINT OF A LINE SEGMENT

Problem 1

Find the midpoint of the line segment with the given endpoints.

$(7, 4)$ and $(9, -1)$

Problem 2

Using the integers -9 to 9 at most one time each, place a digit in each box to create endpoints for two different line segments whose midpoint is $(1, 3)$. One line segment should have a positive slope, and the other should have a negative slope. You may reuse all the integers for each line segment.

$(\square, \square)$ and $(\square, \square)$

Problem 3

Using the integers -9 to 9 at most one time each, place a digit in each box to create endpoints for the longest possible line segment whose midpoint is $(1, 3)$.

$(\square, \square)$ and $(\square, \square)$

Reflection

Problem 1 is a traditional textbook or worksheet problem for finding the midpoint of a line segment. You would expect students to take the endpoints (7, 4) and (9, −1) and find the average value of the *x*- and *y*-coordinates, giving them 8 for the *x*-coordinate from $\frac{(7+9)}{2}$ and 1.5 for the *y*-coordinate from $\frac{(4+(-1))}{2}$. What's important to realize here is that while wrong answers will bring your attention to potential misconceptions, correct answers won't necessarily guarantee that students deeply understand what they're doing.

Consider Problem 2, which prevents students from remaining in the Chinese Room (see Chapter One) and immediately using the midpoint formula. They must instead begin by determining which digits they want to use to solve the problem. First, they have to consider how to select endpoints that will define a line segment with a midpoint at (1, 3). Then, they have to think about how the endpoints determine the line segment's slope. Perhaps you can already imagine students struggling with this, which makes you question how deep their understanding is.

Students might approach Problem 2 visually by using a coordinate plane and labeling (1, 3). Then they'd try to find two points that were equally far apart from (1, 3) but didn't repeat the same digit. Alternatively, they might approach it algebraically, thinking about what two numbers have an average of 1 and what two numbers have an average of 3. Either way, this Open Middle problem will provide you with information about how your students think about midpoints.

Eventually, they should find a line segment with either a positive or a negative slope. For example, students might begin with the endpoints (0, 1) and (2, 5), whose line segment has a positive slope. Then they'll have to think about how to find a line segment with a negative slope. Students might continue to guess and check, which may reflect perseverance but weak understanding. Hopefully, students would use their conceptual understanding to make this process easier. They might realize that changing an endpoint's y-value affects the line segment's slope or that swapping either the x- or y-coordinates would result in a line segment of identical length, just reflected across the line $x = 1$ or $y = 3$, depending on which coordinates they swapped.

Problem 3 challenges students even further, as they have to consider what factors affect a line segment's length and determine how to make the longest line segment. Think about how giving students this Open Middle problem would allow you to walk around the room with X-ray vision and see what they understood or what misconceptions they had. There would likely be opportunities for rich conversation. For example, students might realize that an endpoint such as $(-9, -8)$ would make the line segment longer, but soon they'd realize that they couldn't make a corresponding endpoint using the available digits. Alternatively, students might start with a line segment with endpoints of $(-9, -8)$ and $(8, 9)$. Then they may realize that the midpoint is not $(1, 3)$ and start transforming the line segment until it is the midpoint. Eventually they might start debating whether $(-7, -2)$ and $(9, 8)$ form a longer line segment than $(-6, -3)$ and $(8, 9)$. Visually, it isn't easy to determine which one is longer (see Figure 2.2), and you can probably imagine a debate breaking out among three groups that concluded either the first line segment was longer, the second line segment was longer, or that they were equal in length.

Imagine the rich data you will hear about what skills, misconceptions, and problem approaches students have. What's important to realize is that while everyone will start with the same problem and should end with the same answer, there are a variety of ways to solve it. For example, students could use graph paper to draw the line segments and then use a ruler to measure which one was longer. They might instead use the Pythagorean theorem to calculate the distance between the points. Alternatively, students might also see the line segments as the diagonal of two rectangles with the same

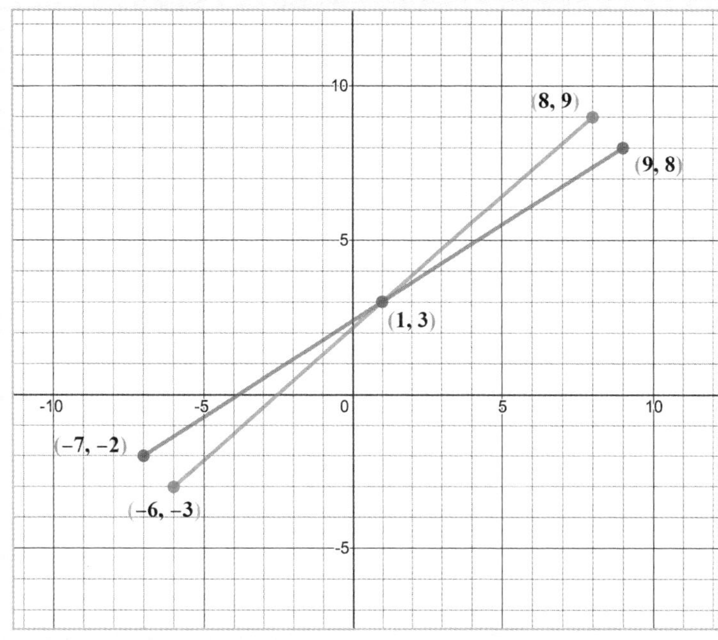

FIGURE 2.2

Which line segment is longer?

(Powered by Desmos)

perimeter (rectangles that measure 10 by 16 and 12 by 14 both have a perimeter of 52 units). In that case, they could use their conceptual understanding to realize that as rectangles with the same perimeter become more like a square (meaning the lengths of the sides become closer together in value), the diagonal gets shorter. Ultimately, all of these reasoning options should lead students to the conclusion that with this problem's restrictions, the longest line segment they can make with a midpoint at $(1, 3)$ has endpoints at $(-7, -2)$ and $(9, 8)$.

Keep reading for more examples or go to page 48 to continue book.

ALGEBRA 2 EXAMPLE
MULTIPLYING COMPLEX NUMBERS

Problem 1

Multiply the binomials.

$$(3+4i)(2+3i)$$

Problem 2

Using the integers −9 to 9 at most one time each, fill in the boxes twice: once to make a positive real number product and once to make a negative real number product. You may reuse all the integers for each product.

$$\left(\square+\square i\right)\left(\square+\square i\right)$$

Problem 3

Using the integers −9 to 9 at most one time each, fill in the boxes to make a real number product with the greatest value.

$$\left(\square+\square i\right)\left(\square+\square i\right)$$

» Reflection

Problem 1 is a traditional problem for multiplying complex numbers. While students may certainly make a mistake with this problem, such as forgetting which terms combine or incorrectly multiplying one or more terms together, solving it correctly (perhaps by using a graphing calculator) and getting $-6+17i$ would not guarantee that they deeply understood what they were doing.

When beginning Problem 2, students may randomly pick four integers to fill the boxes. This is where the Open Middle problem will begin to give you valuable information. If students randomly pick four integers, they are likely to get a product that is not a real number. For example, if students choose digits to create the expression $(3+4i)(2+5i)$, it will simplify to become $-14+23i$, which is a complex number. Some students might think it's impossible to get a real number product without repeating digits. Alternatively, if students think that an answer like $-14+23i$ *is* one of the real number products (possibly the negative real number product) and are ready to find the other, it's a great point to pause and have a conversation about what a real number is.

Eventually, students will have to realize that for the product to be a real number, the i terms will need to be additive inverses of one another. For example, if students chose digits to make the expression $(3+6i)(2+-4i)$, it will be equivalent to $6+-12i+12i+24$. Since the terms $-12i$ and $12i$ are additive inverses, their sum will be zero and the expression will equal 30, making it a positive real number product. Once students have found their first real number product and are looking for the other product, you'll get even more rich information. The method students use to find the opposite real number solution will tell you much about their conceptual understanding.

If your students continue to guess and check, picking random integers, it may mean they have weak understandings. Ideally, students will realize that changing the signs of the digits in one of the binomials will give a real number product with the opposite value, because they are essentially multiplying everything by negative one. For example, changing the expression $(3+6i)(2+-4i)$ to become $(-3-6i)(2+-4i)$ results in $-6+12i+-12i+-24$. However, changing the signs of the integers in *both* of the binomials will give them the same product, because they are essentially multiplying everything by negative one twice. For example, $(-3-6i)(-2+4i)$ results in $6+-12i+12i+24$.

Problem 3 requires even more thinking. You would hope that students would build upon their experiences with Problem 2 and pause to think strategically about what integers to choose. They should realize that they still need partial products that form additive inverses (such as $-12i$ and $12i$) but this time want constants and coefficients with greater absolute values. Imagine the conversations students will have as they debate what the greatest real number product is. For example, when I created this problem, I believed the greatest possible product to be $(6+8i)(3+-4i)=50$. It was many months before I came back to try the problem again and got $(9+6i)(6+-4i)=78$. It was still another two months before I realized that I couldn't do $(9+6i)(6+-4i)$ because I used 6 twice. Finally, I found that $(9+-6i)(6+4i)$ and $(-9+6i)(-6+-4i)=78$ would both give me 78 without breaking the rules. This is a very humbling process! Open Middle problems like this help you authentically understand what your students really know. They have low floors, which allow everyone to enter into the problem, but also high ceilings that challenge even the most eager students.

Keep reading for more examples or go to page 48 to continue book.

TRIGONOMETRY AND PRE-CALCULUS EXAMPLE
EVALUATING TRIGONOMETRIC FUNCTIONS

Problem 1

Evaluate.

$$\sin\left(\frac{\pi}{3}\right)$$

Problem 2

Using the digits 1 to 9 at most one time each, place a digit in each box to make five true number sentences. You may reuse all the digits for each number sentence.

$$\sin\left(\frac{\square\pi}{\square}\right)=1$$

Problem 3

Using the digits 1 to 9 at most one time each, place a digit in each box so that the function has the greatest possible value.

$$\sin\left(\frac{\square\pi}{\square}\right)=\frac{\sqrt{\square}}{\square}$$

Reflection

Problem 1 is a traditional sine function problem. Students might solve it by using memorized values, using a table of trigonometric values such as the one in Table 2.1 to find that $\sin\left(\frac{\pi}{3}\right)=\frac{\sqrt{3}}{2}$, or by interpreting the sine function in the context of a triangle with angles of 30°, 60°, and 90°. The ratio of the sides would then be $1:\sqrt{3}:2$ and also lead to a value of $\frac{\sqrt{3}}{2}$. If students get Problem 1 wrong, you'll know there are some potential misconceptions, but if students answer the problem correctly, you won't be sure that they understand. Instead, they might be stuck in the Chinese Room (see Chapter One), looking for values in a table that make it appear like they know what they are doing, even though they feel lost.

θ	0°	30°	45°	60°	90°	180°	270°	360°
	0	$\frac{\pi}{6}$	$\frac{\pi}{4}$	$\frac{\pi}{3}$	$\frac{\pi}{2}$	π	$\frac{3\pi}{2}$	2π
sin θ	0	$\frac{1}{2}$	$\frac{\sqrt{2}}{2}$	$\frac{\sqrt{3}}{2}$	1	0	-1	0
cos θ	1	$\frac{\sqrt{3}}{2}$	$\frac{\sqrt{2}}{2}$	$\frac{1}{2}$	0	-1	0	1
tan θ	0	$\frac{\sqrt{3}}{3}$	1	$\sqrt{3}$	Undefined	0	Undefined	0

TABLE 2.1

Trigonometric values

Problem 2 can reveal more student thinking. If students have weak understandings when beginning this problem and only know how to evaluate a trigonometric function by using a table of values, they may conclude that there is only one true number sentence: $\sin\left(\frac{1\pi}{2}\right)=1$.

This is where the requirement of five solutions (out of the six possible solutions) is necessary. There are two ways students might find other solutions, one of which is more important from my perspective than the other. First, they might realize that equivalent fractions to $\frac{1\pi}{2}$, such as $\frac{2\pi}{4}$,

$\frac{3\pi}{6}$, and $\frac{4\pi}{8}$, will all result in a value of 1. This is useful to know, but what I really want to determine is whether students understand that sine is a periodic function. By asking for the fifth true number sentence, this problem forces them to think deeper.

They have to realize that there are an infinite number of times where the function will have a value of 1. So, in addition to $\sin\left(\frac{1\pi}{2}\right)=1$, every additional 2π will make it equal to 1 again, leading to $\sin\left(\frac{1\pi}{2}+x\left(2\pi\right)\right)=1$, as long as x is an integer. This will allow them to create two additional answers with the available digits: $\frac{5\pi}{2}$ and $\frac{9\pi}{2}$.

Problem 3 gives even more perspective into what students (or authors) really know about sine functions. When I created this problem, I got the answer wrong. I thought that students might think the answer was $\sin\left(\frac{5\pi}{6}\right)=\frac{\sqrt{1}}{2}$. I had a hunch that this wasn't the greatest possible value, though, and after more attempts got $\sin\left(\frac{4\pi}{6}\right)=\frac{\sqrt{3}}{2}$. I was proud of how I found an equivalent fraction to $\frac{2\pi}{3}$ to make it work. Unfortunately, it wasn't until I started using the problem with others that I was aware that an even greater value could be made. A colleague wisely set the function's value equal to 1 using an equivalent expression of $\frac{\sqrt{4}}{2}$ (or $\frac{\sqrt{9}}{3}$), and then found the angle that made the equation true. She then chose digits to make $\sin\left(\frac{3\pi}{6}\right)=\frac{\sqrt{4}}{2}$, and her function had a greater value than mine!

I share this story rather than hide it away because it's a beautiful example of what can happen in your classroom as well. I thought I had found the greatest possible value, and when I realized I was wrong, it was a memorable learning experience. This is different from what I had experienced as a student, when it seemed like everything that could be known about mathematics already was. Open Middle problems like Problem 3 add excitement to math class because students feel like trailblazers who discover connections in mathematics for the first time.

Keep reading for more examples or go to page 48 to continue book.

CALCULUS EXAMPLE

EVALUATING DEFINITE INTEGRALS

Problem 1

Solve.

$$\int_{2}^{6} x^{3}\,dx$$

Problem 2

Using the digits 1 to 9 at most one time each, fill in the boxes twice: once to make a positive solution and once to make a negative solution. You may reuse all the digits for each solution.

$$\int_{\square}^{\square} x^{\square}\,dx$$

Problem 3

Using the digits 1 to 9 at most one time each, place a digit in each box to make a solution that is as close to 100 as possible.

$$\int_{\square}^{\square} x^{\square}\,dx$$

Reflection

First-semester calculus students will likely be able to integrate $\int_2^6 x^3\,dx$, by integrating $\int x^3\,dx$ to get $\frac{x^4}{4}+C$. They could then evaluate it at 6 and 2 by substitution and get values of 324 when $x=6$, and 4 when $x=2$. Subtracting those two values gives the solution of 320 for the answer to Problem 1.

What's important to realize is that while wrong answers will bring your attention to students' potential misconceptions, correct answers won't necessarily guarantee that students deeply understand what they're doing. They could be stuck inside of the Chinese Room (see Chapter One) and repeating steps in their notes without deeply understanding what they're doing.

Using an Open Middle problem like Problem 2 will give us better X-ray vision and help spot potential misconceptions more clearly. If students begin the problem by guessing and checking and don't move on to a more advanced strategy, it's likely that they have weak conceptual understanding. We would hope that asking students, "How did you decide which digits to use and where to put them?" would result in conversations about the exponent being irrelevant and how all that matters are the values chosen for the bounds. If the upper bound has a greater value than the lower bound, the answer will be positive. If instead the upper bound has a lesser value than the lower bound, the answer will be negative.

With Problem 3, this thinking is extended even further. Students may begin the problem by guessing and checking, randomly placing digits and integrating to find the value. We'd hope that at some point, this would begin to feel futile and would require students to pause and reflect on how the digits they were choosing might affect the function's value. It might be helpful for students to visualize the area this function describes by using a graph. The region would be bounded by the function they create and the line $y=0$. This would allow students to adjust the bounds until there were roughly 100 square units between the bounds. Figure 2.3, created by Lauren Baucom using Desmos, beautifully illustrates what those square units may look like. For example, if the function's exponent value is 0 or 1, it won't generate a value anywhere close to 100, regardless of the bounds chosen. We'd also hope that students would realize that in general, the farther apart the bounds are, the greater the function's value gets. While not always true, bounds with a difference of more than 1 or 2 often increase the function's value far beyond 100. So, while conceptual understanding might not be enough to completely solve the problem, it can save significant time by greatly narrowing the possibilities to check.

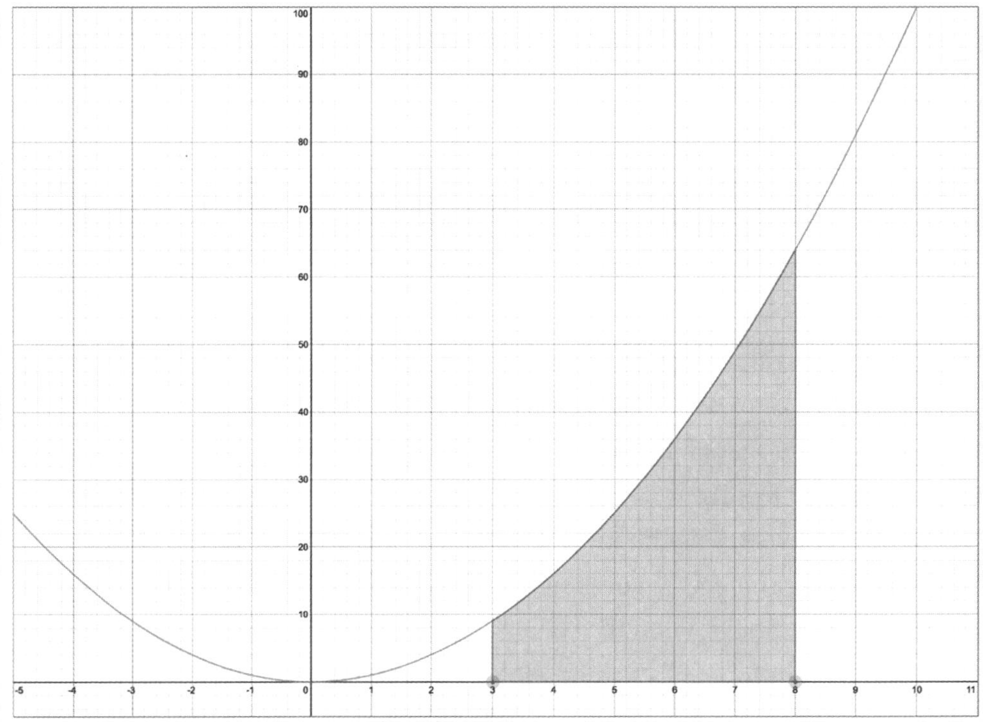

FIGURE 2.3

What does the 100 represent?
(Powered by Desmos)

The important thing about a problem like this is that the journey matters much more than the destination. Whether or not students find the value that's closest to 100 is not nearly as important as the rich conversations and debates they will likely have along the way. This conceptual journey also comes with the added benefit of significant embedded practice. In working on this one problem, students might complete the equivalent of ten or fifteen problems like Problem 1, except we'll also get valuable information about what students know and what they have misconceptions about.

Ultimately, there are two solutions that are very close to 100. The closest possible value is $\int_{6}^{8} x^2\,dx = 98.\overline{6}$, which is $1.\overline{3}$ away from 100. A close second is $\int_{1}^{2} x^9\,dx = 102.3$, which is 2.3 away from 100.

What Are Open Middle Problems?

I hope that trying out the sets of problems has given you a jumbled mix of excitement, curiosity, and concern about using them with your students. Open Middle problems are for all students, not just those who are struggling or those who need more challenge. These problems make learning accessible and are great for differentiation because they tend to have easy entry points yet also make students think deeply. We'll explore how to implement and facilitate them with your students in Chapter Three, but there's a little more to clarify before we move on.

First, a bit of background: My colleague Nanette Johnson and I were inspired to explore the idea of creating problems with open middles after watching Dan Meyer's presentation *Video Games and Making Math More Like Things Students Like* (2014). In his presentation, Dan talked about how math problems, like video games, have a beginning, a middle, and an end that can be open or closed.

Dan used the image in Figure 2.4 to illustrate how most video games have players start each level in the same place and win by completing the same goal. In this way, the beginning and ending are *closed* because they're the same for everyone. What makes the games interesting to play is that there are often many paths you can take from the start to the finish. So, the middle is *open* because what happens between the beginning and ending is up to you. If you had to follow a tedious set of instructions to complete each level, the middle would also be closed, and the game would be much less interesting.

Similarly, most math problems begin with everyone having the same problem and working toward the same answer. As a result, the beginning and ending are closed. What varies is the middle. Sometimes a problem's instructions tell students to complete a problem using a specific method (a closed middle). Other times, there are many possible ways to solve the problem (an open middle). Problems with

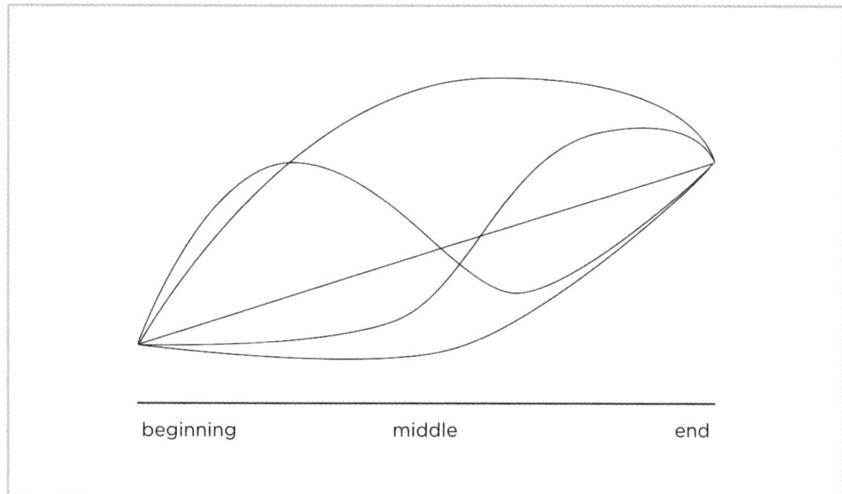

FIGURE 2.4

Visual depiction of problems with a closed beginning, open middle, and closed ending from Dan Meyer

open middles tend to be much more interesting and lead to richer conversations. Dan's framing greatly intrigued Nanette and me, so we tried to make our own math problems, mostly with closed beginnings, open middles, and closed endings.

As colleagues at Downey Unified School District, where we were both math teacher specialists who supported middle and high school math teachers, Nanette and I spent many hours creating and implementing these kinds of problems with students and teachers. We often had eye-opening experiences we wanted to discuss with others. So we created a website called Open Middle to share the problems we made and generate in-person and online discussions. Since then, educators around the world have contributed hundreds of other problems. This book, the problems, and the strategies could not have been made without Nanette and all math educators who create, use, and share Open Middle problems.

Depth of Knowledge

Up to this point, we've been referring to the sets of problems as Problems 1, 2, and 3. Now that we have a firmer grasp of the differences among these problems, it may be helpful to relate this framework to the widely utilized Depth of Knowledge classification.

Depth of Knowledge (DOK) is a way of classifying questions that's based on how deep a person's knowledge must be to answer them. The higher a problem's DOK level is, the deeper a person's understanding must be.

Depth of Knowledge was first described by Norman L. Webb of the University of Wisconsin–Madison in 1997 when he was looking at standardized assessments and noticed a gap between the level of understanding described by content standards and the level of understanding assessments used to measure those content standards. This gap is similar to the one I experienced with my own classes. Students were labeled as proficient or advanced because I taught them strategies to help them answer superficial questions, but they didn't have the conceptual understanding the standards required.

Webb developed four levels for classifying tasks by their Depth of Knowledge:

1. *Recall*: Recall of a fact, information, or procedure.
2. *Skill/Concept*: Use of information, conceptual knowledge, procedures, two or more steps, etc.
3. *Strategic Thinking*: Requires reasoning, developing a plan or sequence of steps; has some complexity; more than one possible answer . . .
4. *Extended Thinking*: Requires an investigation; time to think and process multiple conditions of the problem or task . . . (1999, 3).

Depth of Knowledge has been useful as a tool to describe the increasing levels of understanding that students need to solve Open Middle problems. So, another way to describe Problems 1, 2, and 3 is by their Depth of Knowledge levels, which are 1, 2, and 3, respectively.

For example, with the three one-step equations we compared at the beginning of this chapter, Problem 1, $21+x=70$, was DOK 1. To solve it, students could recall a procedure for solving one-step equations and find the solution with relative ease.

Problem 1

Solve for x.

$$21+x=70$$

Problem 2

Using the digits 1 to 9 at most one time each, fill in the boxes twice: once to make a positive solution and once to make a negative solution. You may reuse all the digits for each solution.

$$\square\square+x=\square\square$$

Problem 3

Using the digits 1 to 9 at most one time each, place a digit in each box to make a solution that is as close to 100 as possible.

$$\square\square+x=\square\square$$

Problem 2 was about finding one positive solution and one negative solution and was DOK 2. Students needed to use conceptual understanding, pattern recognition, or both to solve it. The procedure for solving a one-step equation no longer worked when they were not given the numbers.

Finally, Problem 3 was DOK 3. Students had to think strategically about how their digit choices affected the value of *x*. Guessing and checking was no longer an efficient strategy, and conceptual understanding was required. A casual way to describe DOK 3 comes from Nolan Bushnell, founder of video game company Atari, who said that "the best games are easy to learn and difficult to master." Similarly, Open Middle problems at DOK 3 are often easy to begin and challenging to find the optimal answer for.

You may be wondering about what DOK 4 would look like in mathematics. Generally, these are represented by mathematical modeling and authentic real-world applications of mathematics. These bigger problems require students to account for a variety of information and constraints and, while valuable, are not a focus of this book. In general, I'm less concerned about the differences between the Depth of Knowledge levels than I am about math teachers using problems beyond DOK 1, especially problems that have open middles.

Connections to Other Kinds of Problems

Over the years that we've been creating and using Open Middle problems, we've learned a great deal from other teachers, researchers, and colleagues' work around what makes for effective question and problem types, especially from the following sources.

Marian Small

Marian Small has long talked about the value of making parts of questions open. In her book *Good Questions: Great Ways to Differentiate Mathematics Instruction*, Small says that "a question is open when it is framed in such a way that a variety of responses or approaches are possible" (2009, 6). Framed in the language of problem beginnings, middles, and endings, Small defines a question as open when it has both an open middle and an open ending, and she values how open questions make "the mathematical conversation . . . richer" (7). Small emphasizes the use of "replacing a number with a blank," which allows students to choose numbers for themselves (8). "For example, instead of asking how many students there are altogether if there are 25 in one class and 31 in another, students could be asked to choose two numbers for the two class sizes and determine the total number in both classes" (8).

Marcy Cook

Marcy Cook has created math problem task cards that look very similar to Open Middle problems. The task cards generally involve boxes that have to be filled with the digits 0 to 9. They also begin with the same problem and end with the same answer, while allowing flexibility for how to solve them. In that way, they also have open middles as well as closed beginnings and endings.

Her math problem task cards differ from Open Middle problems in small but important details. Usually, there are ten boxes, which require students to use all ten digits every time. This structure may change students' approach from strategically determining which digits are best to determining which digits go where so they find the one correct answer for each box.

SmudgedMath

SmudgedMath, created by Peter Liljedahl, transforms regular math tasks by replacing portions of them with smudges, as if some of the problem were accidently smudged. Students are not provided with information about what is under the smudge, so it could be anything, including a number, a variable, a diagram, an operation, or combinations of them. The goal isn't for students to uncover what was smudged but rather to open up the possibilities and allow students to explore what could have been.

As a result, students may have conversations that are similar to those they'd have with Open Middle problems, giving the teacher clearer insight into students' misconceptions. SmudgedMath problems are different from Open Middle problems because there is intentionally less structure about what is missing (or smudged). The problems are generally not about finding the right answer and are more an exploration about what is possible.

Now that you have a better understanding of what Open Middle problems look like, where the idea for Open Middle came from, and some similar approaches in mathematics education, let's start talking about the process of using Open Middle problems with your students.

REFLECTION QUESTIONS

Here are some questions for you to reflect on by yourself, with your colleagues, or on social media using the #OpenMiddleBook hashtag.

- How can students still have misconceptions if they are able to correctly complete an entire worksheet of problems like Problem 1?
- What encouraging and discouraging emotions might students feel when doing Open Middle problems like Problems 2 and 3 after a lifetime of exposure to problems like Problem 1? Why would they feel that way?
- Mathematics has traditionally been about getting correct answers, so why do you think the journey in completing Open Middle problems is often more important than the destination?

CHAPTER THREE
WHAT DO WE NEED TO DO BEFORE USING A PROBLEM WITH STUDENTS?

When I first started teaching, my students spent much of each class solving problems I chose from my textbook. I rarely thought about the conversations I hoped would take place. Discussions tended to be unremarkable and primarily focused on the steps students took to solve the problems.

As I became more experienced and began incorporating richer problems, I noticed that occasionally students would stumble into powerful conversations that helped them develop deeper understandings and take pleasure in the beauty of mathematics. It was hard to predict when these moments would take place, so I savored them when they happened.

Over a decade later, I started to realize that these moments could be orchestrated and did not have to be random. I realized that with strategic planning, I could choose a problem and craft questions that would spark these conversations on a regular basis. These discussions gave me deeper insight into students' understandings as well as their misconceptions and resulted in more students who loved learning mathematics.

I wish I had known how to strategically plan out lessons earlier in my career, but I'm glad I better understand it now. Planned-out lessons frequently lead to great experiences that help students develop deeper connections around mathematics. The strategies I use take more work to prepare, but it's well worth the time because I find that students have a better experience if I've thought about the different ways they could solve the problem, where they might get stuck, and their possible correct and incorrect answers.

I've organized Chapters Three and Four into sections based on questions we might discuss if we were planning to use an Open Middle problem with your students. In this chapter we'll walk through the planning process, and then we'll talk about how to implement the planned-out problem with students in Chapter Four. You can certainly adjust these steps based on how you intend to use a problem and how much time you have, but I'll break everything down into detailed descriptions because I want you to have the big picture. To help make this conversation as concrete as possible, I'll use a single problem as an example throughout both chapters, so you can see what the steps would look like.

Let's begin by imagining that you and I are in your classroom, talking about a lesson we are planning to teach together early next week. You started a unit on solving linear equations in one variable earlier this week and have found that while most students have been able to solve basic problems, you're unsure about whether they are just repeating the steps in their notes or whether they have conceptual understanding of what they're doing. A traditional problem for this concept might look like this:

> Solve for x.
>
> $$4x + 3 = 2x + 7$$

You know you want to ask a richer question, but you're not sure where to start. Let's talk about it.

How Should We Get Started?

It's important to realize that students will experience a range of emotions when working on their first Open Middle problems. Some will feel the joy of having a problem they can think deeply about while others will experience anxiety and frustration when math no longer means repeating the steps in their notes. We'll be able to empathize with that range of emotions because we probably felt similarly when working on our first Open Middle problems (like those in Chapter Two). So let's begin slowly and give students positive first experiences with these problems. As an example of what *not* to do, let me share a lesson I learned the hard way.

When I was just beginning to use these kinds of problems with students, I tried out this fifth-grade problem on subtracting mixed numbers with a class of eighth graders. Spend a few minutes working on it now and then continue reading.

> Using the digits 1 to 9 at most one time each, place a digit in each box to create the smallest difference possible.
>
> 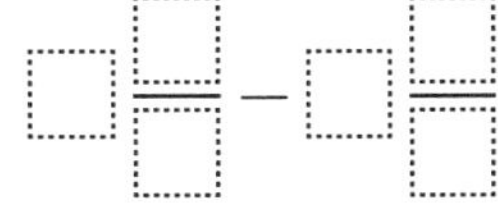

As you may have noticed, the problem is much more challenging than a typical subtracting mixed numbers problem. I figured that this problem would still be fine because these students had learned about subtracting mixed numbers more than three years earlier. Oh, was that a bad assumption! Students' struggle with the mathematics was compounded by their unfamiliarity with the format of Open Middle problems (such as filling in boxes with digits) and their inexperience with persevering. It was not a fun time.

I came to realize that I was too ambitious for my first attempt. Instead, I should have started with a problem on a concept that students would understand yet also not be able to solve on their first attempt. For example, consider this problem:

> Using the digits 1 to 9 at most one time each, place a digit in each box to create a sum that is as close to 1,000 as possible.
>
> 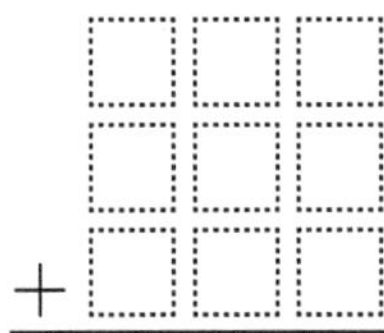

What's great about this problem is that very few children or adults get it right the first time, yet very few give up either because it doesn't feel unreasonable. By starting with a problem like this, students develop some useful understandings about Open Middle problems including:

- It's probably going to take many attempts to solve the problem, even with a concept they understand.
- Almost everyone takes multiple attempts, so not getting it right on their first try doesn't mean they're not smart.
- There are multiple methods to get the same correct answer.
- Discussing the problem with others can be helpful.
- Problem solving can actually be fun.

So, before we use grade-level-appropriate problems with your students, we should ensure that they have early successes. You might initially worry that we don't have time for a problem that's not in your content standards, but these first impressions are so important that that we don't have time *not* to do it. If we invest time now to prepare students for this type of problem solving, students will look forward to future problems, and facilitating those problems will be much easier.

> IF WE INVEST TIME NOW TO PREPARE STUDENTS FOR THIS TYPE OF PROBLEM SOLVING, STUDENTS WILL LOOK FORWARD TO FUTURE PROBLEMS, AND FACILITATING THOSE PROBLEMS WILL BE MUCH EASIER.

Ideally, we would invite students to work on a problem like this during the first days of school to set the tone that math will be both challenging and fun. However, since we're starting midyear, we should squeeze one or two introductory problems in before our grade-level lesson, to familiarize students with the process. If we don't have enough time during class, we could assign problems like the one on adding three-digit numbers for homework and discuss them in class. Having this positive initial experience will set the tone for all future Open Middle problems.

It might take facilitating a few problems like this for students to get the hang of the process, but once they know what to do, we can shift toward problems that are part of your standards. At that point, students will be less apprehensive because the experience will be more familiar and remind them of something they enjoyed. (I'll talk about where we can get hundreds of free problems to choose from later on, in Chapter Five.)

When Would We Want to Use an Open Middle Problem?

Open Middle problems work best as substitutes for traditional procedural practice problems (like worksheets, classwork, or homework) or as formative assessments to determine what students really understand. They are less ideal as an introduction to a new topic, because students who have not learned how to solve a basic problem will often be unable to handle these more challenging problems. Generally, the only time we would want to use an Open Middle problem at the beginning of a unit is as a short formative assessment to see what students already know.

As an example, here's how we might incorporate one into our classwork. If we were teaching students about one-step equations, instead of using a worksheet containing thirty traditional one-step equations, we might give students only four problems from the worksheet to assess whether they know the procedures. Once we determined that they had the computational skill to solve surface-level problems, we could have students work on an Open Middle problem, which could help students grow while practicing their skills and give us far more valuable information than another twenty-six problems that were very similar to what they had already done.

Alternatively, we might use an Open Middle problem on an assessment. Realize that if we don't use Open Middle problems on assessments, then we might be collecting data that doesn't truly represent what students know. That being said, don't make the same mistake I made and put Open Middle problems on an assessment without having ever used them in class! Students need familiarity with working on these types of problems before you put them on assessments. Using Open Middle problems with students ahead of time will help you distinguish between students who are confused about the mathematics and those who are unfamiliar with the problem's format.

How Do We Choose a Problem?

The first thing to think about when choosing an Open Middle problem is determining what our concern is. In this case, because we're toward the beginning of a unit on solving linear equations in one variable, our concern is that students might appear to understand the procedures for solving a linear equation, but we're unsure about whether they conceptually understand what they're doing or are just robotically repeating the steps. So we're looking for a problem that will give us X-ray vision and help us determine what they know more clearly.

Next, we should look to see what Open Middle problems have already been created for this standard. As I mentioned earlier, hundreds of problems have already been created and are available for free online (more on this in Chapter Five). So if a problem has already been created for this standard, using it will be our best option because the problem will come with hints, answers, and occasionally helpful comments from teachers who've used it with their students. Otherwise, we'll have to create our own (more on making our own problems in Chapter Five as well).

Once we've figured out what problems are available, we'll have to figure out which one best meets our needs. For example, consider the following three similar problems on solving linear equations in one variable. It's important that we spend time solving each of them to determine if they're truly a good fit. I say this because I've accidentally chosen problems that looked good at a glance but actually incorporated skills students hadn't learned yet, didn't lead to the conversations I wanted students to have, or were so hard that I didn't understand how to solve them. This has even happened when *I've* made the problem!

So, while we could certainly take an Open Middle problem and try to solve it for the first time when we're with your students, I wouldn't recommend it. I've found that investing time early on in the process consistently produces high-quality classroom conversations and experiences. So take some time to try solving these problems so that we can decide which one to move forward with.

Option A

> Using the digits 1 to 9 at most one time each, place a digit in each box to create an equation with a solution that's as close to zero as possible.
>
> $\square x + \square = \square x + \square$

Option B

> Using the digits 1 to 9 at most *two times* each, place a digit in each box to create an equation with no solution.
>
> $\square x + \square = \square x + \square$

Option C

> Using the digits 1 to 9 at most one time each, place a digit in each box to create two equations: one where x has a positive value and one where x has a negative value. You may reuse all the digits for each equation.
>
> $\square x + \square = \square x + \square$

While all three problems may lead to valuable learning and conversations, to decide which one we should pick we need to focus back on what our original concern was. We wondered if students might appear to know how to solve linear equations when in actuality they are just robotically repeating procedures without conceptual understanding.

Option A will certainly help students focus on how the coefficients and constants affect the solution's value, but it is a Level 3 problem and might be too rigorous for our purposes because finding a solution that's as close to zero as possible is quite challenging.

Option B will help students see the connections between linear equations and systems of linear equations. While that would make for an interesting conversation with many discoveries, it doesn't align as well with our concern of determining whether students have conceptual understanding of solving linear equations in one variable. It is Level 2.

Finally, Option C has some of the same features as Option A because it will also help students focus on how the coefficients and constants affect the solution's value. However, by asking for a positive and a negative solution instead of one that's as close to zero as possible, it is Level 2 and seems better as an entry-level problem because there are many possible answers. So, I recommend moving forward with Option C. If you like one or both of the other problems, we could certainly use either of them at a later point.

To be clear, we don't always have to begin by showing students a Level 1 problem first, then a Level 2, and then a Level 3. However, if we're not sure about what students know, it's generally better to start off with a lower-level problem and then follow up with more advanced problems once it's clear that they are ready for more challenge.

How Do We Prepare to Use the Problem?

With our chosen Open Middle problem handy, let's plan how we hope the problem will unfold over the course of the lesson. Planning doesn't mean that every moment will be scripted. Rather, planning will help us understand what moments are possible and allow us to intentionally guide students toward our favorite discoveries and conversations that we might have missed otherwise.

In general, we should follow the steps laid out by Margaret (Peg) Smith and Mary Kay Stein in their book *Five Practices for Orchestrating*

Productive Mathematical Discussions (2011). I consider this book to be the bible of how to facilitate discussions around virtually any rich math task. In a related article, Smith, Hughes, Engle, and Stein explained that to engineer productive mathematical discussions, we should

1. anticipate student responses to the problem they are working on;
2. monitor students' work on and engagement with the task;
3. select particular students to present their mathematical work;
4. sequence the student responses to be displayed in a specific order; and
5. connect the students' responses to one another and to key mathematical ideas. (2009, 550)

The process begins with the first practice: anticipating student responses. Here, we'll invest time to think about all the ways students might correctly or incorrectly solve a problem. This anticipation will reduce our stress and anxiety during the lesson because we'll be more familiar with what might happen.

While students are working during the lesson, we'll do the next three practices: monitor students' work, select particular students to present their work, and sequence their responses in a specific order. We'll have an easier time doing these practices because of the time we spent working on the problem and anticipating how students might approach it. We'll come into the lesson with ideas about conversations we can have to address what students know or don't know. These ideas will help form our mathematical goal, which we will use to decide which student work to highlight and the order in which we'll want the work to be shared to orchestrate a productive discussion. We'll be walking around the room, writing down what students are doing, selecting the work that will best suit our needs, and thinking about how we can sequence that work to build a mathematical story.

Anticipating, monitoring, selecting, and sequencing will set us up for the final practice, where we'll facilitate a conversation to help students make connections among the shared student work and with the concepts they are learning about. During the conversation, we'll ask questions that will tell us more about what students know and give them opportunities to make deeper connections.

Of these five practices, I believe that the most important is anticipating student responses. When my lessons haven't gone like I had hoped (which still happens often), it has almost always been because I didn't adequately anticipate how students would solve the problem. I figured that everyone would solve the problem just like I did, and when that did not happen, I had to spend precious classroom minutes uncovering and understanding what students did and planning my next steps. This in-class scramble has happened most often when kids got stuck in places I had not anticipated, but it has also happened when they solved the problem using methods I hadn't considered.

It's not my intention to say that these unexpected moments are bad. For sure, they make teaching interesting. What I am trying to say is that sometimes these unanticipated mistakes were so prevalent that I wished I had been aware of them before the lesson so I could have strategically addressed them in every class. Similarly, there may have been students in other classes with the same creative ways of solving the problem, but because I was unaware that the methods existed, I was less prepared to incorporate them into the classroom conversation.

Understanding the many ways students might solve a problem or get stuck will reduce our stress and anxiety and help us spend less time during the lesson figuring out what they're doing. To capture information about how students might solve the problem, we'll turn our list of strategies (both correct and incorrect) into a chart called a

Student Strategy Tracker, which we can use to record students' strategies as we walk around the class. This chart was inspired by Smith and Stein's tool for monitoring student's explorations (2011, 552). See Figure 3.1 for an example of what the Student Strategy Tracker might look like. You can download a version at http://www.robertkaplinsky.com/sst.

The "Strategy" column is for the name of the correct or incorrect strategy students might use and any information about that strategy that we'll need to refresh our memory if we forget what it was. Sometimes there will be days, weeks, or longer between planning a problem and using it, so any details about the strategy will help refresh our memory. The "Student Name(s) and Notes" column is for the names of the students who used those strategies and any notes about what they did. The "Order" column is for the order in which we want students to share the strategies to achieve our goal (more on determining the order in Chapter Four). Prior to using the problem in class, we'll want to fill in our Student Strategy Tracker with the strategies we anticipate students using. We won't need to use the "Student Name(s) and Notes" and "Order" columns until the lesson begins.

Strategy	Student Name(s) and Notes	Order
Strategy 1		
Strategy 2		
Strategy 3		
Strategy 4		
Strategy 5		

FIGURE 3.1

Student Strategy Tracker

Let's return to the problem we've chosen to anticipate the many ways students might solve it so that we can jot them down on our Student Strategy Tracker. I have found that when I can think of only one correct way to solve a problem or no ways students will get stuck, it's usually a bad sign because I'm underprepared for what students are going to do. This is why I greatly prefer to work with other educators when anticipating how students might solve problems. My colleagues often approach problems in ways I hadn't considered. This pre-lesson discussion simultaneously saves me time and better prepares me for using the problem with students.

So, let's spend some time together solving the problem we've chosen. We should try to use as many correct strategies as we can think of and consider where students might get stuck. Once we've each found all the ways we can think of, let's continue the conversation.

> Using the digits 1 to 9 at most one time each, place a digit in each box to create two equations: one where x has a positive value and one where x has a negative value. You may reuse all the digits for each equation.
>
> $\square x + \square = \square x + \square$

Let's compare the various ways we've thought about for how students might solve the problem or get stuck. My hope is that you will have ideas I had not thought of or vice versa, which is all the more reason to do this process with other educators when possible. In this case, I thought of three ways students might solve the problem: guessing and checking, switching the constants, and switching the coefficients.

If students guess and check, they will begin by randomly placing a digit in each of the boxes to get their first solution, which will be either positive or negative. Then, to get the other solution, they will continue to randomly place a digit in each box until they find a solution with the opposite sign. For example, they may get $1x + 2 = 3x + 4$ for their first equation. This equation's solution is $x = -1$. Next, they might try $1x + 2 = 3x + 5$, $1x + 2 = 3x + 6$, and $1x + 2 = 3x + 7$ to see if adding one to a constant will change the solution's sign. Alternatively, they might pick four new random digits like $5x+7=2x+9$.

If they are purely guessing and checking, this process might continue for a while until they accidently find a solution of the opposite sign. Hopefully, we'll instead see students building their conceptual understanding through each additional attempt. If not, it may show us that while they may understand the procedures for solving the problem, they have limited conceptual understanding of how the coefficients and constants affect the solution's value.

Another possibility is that students might solve the problem by picking digits randomly for their first equation but use their conceptual understanding to pick digits for their second equation. For example, they may begin with $1x+2=3x+4$, which again has a solution of $x= -1$. However, at this point they might pause and think strategically about what to do for their next equation. Students might realize that swapping the digits for either the coefficients or the constants will result in a solution of the opposite sign. For example, $3x+2=1x+4$ (swapping the coefficients) and $1x+4=3x+2$ (swapping the constants) both have solutions of $x=1$. If we see students using either of these strategies, it will be wonderful because it's a sign that students have both procedural skills and conceptual understanding.

WE SHOULD PREPARE FOR STUDENTS' STRUGGLES BY HAVING INTERVENTIONS READY TO USE AS NEEDED, NOT BY PRE-TEACHING THE SKILLS WE EXPECT STUDENTS TO STRUGGLE WITH.

Next, let's talk about where students might get stuck. My hunch is that the most common mistakes will be students forgetting how to solve a basic linear equation in one variable or forgetting integer and fraction operations. These are common challenges we'll face when teaching any class of students. We should prepare for students' struggles by having interventions ready to use as needed, not by pre-teaching the skills we expect students to struggle with.

As Juli K. Dixon, Lisa A. Brooks, and Melissa R. Carli explain in their book *Making Sense of Mathematics for Teaching the Small Group,* we want to use "just-in-time scaffolding," not "just-in-case scaffolding" (2019, 11). So we do not want to start class by telling kids something like, "Today we'll be doing a problem that will require you to solve linear equations as well as work with integers and fractions. Let's review how to do these skills."

While it might be more convenient for us to begin each class this way and kids might progress through the problem more smoothly, much of what we see could be artificial. We should aim to give students the least amount of help they need, only when they need it. One metaphor that helps me think about how we help students is that of a bench presser and a spotter. Students are doing the bench pressing, and our job is to spot them. While too little help is dangerous, too much help when they don't need it results in us getting stronger, not them.

Helping them before they need it also makes assessing what students know more challenging, as students might be able to robotically repeat what they just saw during the pre-teaching without authentically understanding what they're doing. Ideally, we'll want to wait until students realize they don't understand something and crave the skills they need so that they can solve the problem. Dan Meyer uses a beautiful metaphor for this craving when he says, "If math is the aspirin, then how do you create the headache?" (2015). If students feel real need for the mathematics first, then they'll be able to apply the new skills immediately and will better understand why they're useful, instead of yet again learning math skills for some random time in the future when they might come in handy.

Now, with ideas for how students might correctly solve the problem, it's time to return to our Student Strategy Tracker and fill it in with the potential strategies and mistakes. Any additional ways you or your colleagues found should be added to the Student Strategy Tracker so we're even more prepared for anticipating what students might do. We should leave one or more rows blank to record strategies that emerge that we didn't anticipate. When filled in, it should look something like Figure 3.2.

As a result of the time we spent anticipating how students might solve the problem, we'll be able to use the Student Strategy Tracker to keep track of students' progress along paths we're already familiar with. While we're walking around the classroom and monitoring what students are doing, we might think of ourselves as directors who are creating a movie about solving linear equations in one variable. We will already have an idea about what scenes (or in this case, strategies) we can choose from, but what we need to think about next is the message we want to convey. Depending on which strategies students share, the order in which they present them, and the questions we ask students to think about, students will come away with different understandings. So let's think about the choices.

What Understandings Do We Want Students to Gain from the Problem?

Even though every student will be working on the same problem, the classroom conversations that follow do not have to be the same. The conversations will shift depending on which student work gets shared and which questions we ask.

For example, if we're frustrated that students keep making the same mistakes, we might choose two or three students who *incorrectly* solved the problem to present their work. Perhaps one student incorrectly solved the linear equation by subtracting twice on the same side of the equals sign. Another student might have made an integer calculation error. A third may have forgotten a variable when rewriting the equation. Then, we would focus the conversation that followed on whose mistake was the most illuminating for helping students clarify

Strategy	Student Name(s) and Notes	Order
Guess and Check (Students randomly place digits in each box until they have both a positive and a negative solution, hopefully with many incorrect attempts.)		
Swapping Constants (Students get their second equation by keeping the coefficients in the same place and swapping the location of the constants.)		
Swapping Coefficients (Students get their second equation by keeping the constants in the same place and swapping the location of the coefficients.)		
Solving Linear Equation Errors (Students can't remember the procedures for solving a linear equation.)		
Fraction or Integer Calculation Errors (Students make mistakes when performing operations on rational numbers.)		

FIGURE 3.2

Student Strategy Tracker that has correct and incorrect strategies filled in.

their own misunderstandings. In this case, our mathematical goal would be to highlight common mistakes so that students could make them less often.

Alternatively, we might begin a classroom conversation by having a student who used a guess-and-check strategy present his or her work first. Most of the class should be able to understand the strategy used, and few students would be lost by the student's explanation. The class would realize that while the student correctly found both a positive and a negative solution, the strategy he or she used was fairly inefficient. Next, we could have students who swapped the coefficients or constants share their work. The hope would be that the rest of the class would now value how efficient these strategies are. In this case, our mathematical goal would be helping students develop conceptual understanding of solving linear equations in one variable and use more efficient strategies.

Picking the second of these two mathematical goals might be best for addressing our concern that students have limited conceptual understanding of solving linear equations in one variable; however, other options we might consider for this or other problems include the following:

- *Begin with the most common method for solving a problem and work toward the least common.* This might work well for a problem on solving systems of linear equations, where there are often multiple methods for solving a problem (such as substitution, elimination, graphing, or using tables of values), yet students stick with the same method every time because they feel most comfortable with it, even if it is not the most efficient for a problem. In this case, our mathematical goal would be to help students feel stronger with other problem-solving methods so that they'd feel comfortable choosing the most appropriate strategy for solving a problem.

- *Begin with the least efficient strategy for solving a problem and work toward the most efficient strategy.* This could work well for a problem where students preferred to repeat an operation over and over to find an answer. They might eventually get the correct answer, but a more advanced strategy like writing a function would save time. In this case, our mathematical goal would be to help them move to more efficient strategies.
- *Begin with a student who solved a problem using a concrete method, then a student who used a representational method, and finally a student who used an abstract method.* This could work well when multiplying binomials, as we could begin with someone who used or drew algebra tiles to represent each of the terms when multiplying. Next, we could have someone share how he or she represented those tiles using an array. Finally, we could have someone who multiplied each of the terms by the others using a procedure explain what he or she did. Often, the visual solutions will help reveal the mathematics in the abstract solutions, and the abstract solutions can help students connect symbolic manipulation with their corresponding physical actions. The conversation would be around how the methods were connected to one another. In this case, our mathematical goal would be to help students develop conceptual understanding and procedural fluency.
- *Begin with a student who solved a problem using an abstract method, then a student who used a representational method, and finally a student who used a concrete method.* This is the reverse of the previous mathematical goal and works well when students already know a procedure but have little conceptual understanding about where it comes from. For example, if students know how to use FOIL when multiplying binomials but do not conceptually understand why it works,

they may be able to complete the problem with symbols but may be challenged by trying to connect their procedural understanding to the representational and concrete methods. In this case, our mathematical goal would be to help students understand where a procedure came from.

With all of these mathematical goals in mind, there are many important takeaways we should reflect on. First, all of these conversations are valuable. In fact, it would be great if we had enough time to talk about each of them. Unfortunately, we have limited classroom minutes, so I recommend picking the mathematical goal that addresses our biggest concern and start there. If we wind up having enough time to incorporate any other conversations, that would be a bonus. For our lesson, I suggest we choose the mathematical goal of helping students develop conceptual understanding of solving linear equations in one variable and begin with a student who used a guess-and-check strategy followed by students who swapped coefficients and constants.

Next, realize that no matter what conversation takes place, students will still be working on the same problem and that portion of the lesson will not change. Also, the time we spent anticipating student responses will make the experience flow much better and reduce our stress and anxiety because we'll be more familiar with what might happen. Our thoughtful planning will even help us feel more comfortable switching mathematical goals mid-lesson if the desire arises.

THE TIME WE SPENT ANTICIPATING STUDENT RESPONSES WILL MAKE THE EXPERIENCE FLOW MUCH BETTER AND REDUCE OUR STRESS AND ANXIETY BECAUSE WE'LL BE MORE FAMILIAR WITH WHAT MIGHT HAPPEN.

With our potential mathematical goals and lesson plan in mind, let's move on to Chapter Four, where we'll address implementing this Open Middle problem and facilitating discussions using the practices from *Five Practices for Orchestrating Productive Mathematical Discussions* (Smith and Stein 2011).

REFLECTION QUESTIONS

Here are some questions for you to reflect on by yourself, with your colleagues, or on social media using the #OpenMiddleBook hashtag.

- Why should we use problems from an earlier grade level when first introducing Open Middle problems to students?
- How could using one or two Open Middle problems instead of dozens of traditional procedural practice problems help students develop deeper understandings and give us richer information about what they know?
- How would spending time anticipating how students might correctly or incorrectly solve a problem reduce our stress and increase the likelihood of having powerful classroom conversations?

CHAPTER FOUR
HOW DO WE USE A PROBLEM WITH STUDENTS?

In Chapter Three, we discussed how to prepare to use an Open Middle problem. It's important to realize that while preparing to use these problems is very valuable, the actual lessons rarely go exactly as we plan. It reminds me of a quote from General Dwight D. Eisenhower: "In preparing for battle I have always found that plans are useless, but planning is indispensable" (1962, 253). So, while students may not solve the problem exactly like we expected or may get stuck in ways we did not think of, the time we spent anticipating what students might do will make us better prepared to handle the unexpected. So, let's talk about how to implement the problem we planned out in Chapter Three with students.

> Using the digits 1 to 9 at most one time each, place a digit in each box to create two equations: one where x has a positive value and one where x has a negative value. You may reuse all the digits for each equation.
>
> $\square x + \square = \square x + \square$

How Do We Get Students Started on the Problem?

When we first use this Open Middle problem, we should have everyone work on the same problem at the same time. Options for sharing the problem include writing the problem on the board, projecting it on a screen, handing it out on a slip of paper, displaying it on a device, or any other form of getting everyone focused on the task at hand.

Next, we want to make sure students understand what's expected of them. Initially, we'll have to explain what to do in great detail. As they become more familiar with the process during the year, we'll spend much less time on this step. For example, most Open Middle problems have requirements that we will need to ensure students understand including:

- Generally, students should fill each box with a single digit or integer.
- Students can use only certain digits or integers (such as −9 to 9, 0 to 9, or 1 to 9).
- They often cannot use a digit or integer more than once.
- They frequently need to find specific kinds of answers, such as a positive and a negative solution, the greatest or least solution, or a solution that's closest to a certain value.

Reviewing these restrictions helps students stay on track and lessens (though rarely eliminates) some issues like using the wrong digits or using the same digit more than once. If we find that those two issues are challenges, we can have students use tiles or pieces of paper with the available digits or integers on them so they can better keep track of what they have to use.

What Happens After We Explain the Directions to Students?

After students understand what the problem is asking them to do, we let them work on it. I'd recommend letting each student begin by working on the problem individually, regardless of what the seating arrangement is. This individual time wasn't something I always utilized, though. When I first began using Open Middle problems, I would let students talk and collaboratively work on the problem right away. Students' conversations made me feel good because it appeared that most kids were engaged and talking about mathematics. In actuality, my impression was only partially true, as what was really happening was more complex.

Eventually I realized that I was primarily paying attention to the details that made me feel like things were going great and dismissing the parts that showed me otherwise. For example, by telling students to talk and work together right away, I put students into a situation where they were talking about a challenging problem that they had spent almost no time working on. The conversations were often superficial because the students barely had any experience with the problem before chatting about it.

Additionally, I found that too often the dominant personality in the group shared his or her thoughts while the students who were more apprehensive sat and listened. Occasionally the dominant student unknowingly shared an incorrect strategy while the other students said nothing. Sometimes students even switched away from their correct strategies after listening to the dominant student because they had not been given enough time to feel confident in their own work! These experiences have helped me shift how I get students started on a problem.

So, after we give students a problem and they understand the directions, we should let them begin individually. We can give them about two to five minutes, but we don't need to time them. Instead, we should walk around the room, observing students, and reading their body language. When students' eyes are on their papers and their pencils are writing, it's a sign that they have more thinking to do. Slowly, students will start putting their pencils down and begin looking around the room. When about 70% of them look ready to talk, we should check back in with them. I've tried waiting until 100% of students were done writing, but that caused different problems because some students were done for quite a while and became distracted.

At this point, I prefer to allow students to work with a partner or as part of a small group of three to four students. We can tell students that they can choose between continuing to work on their own and talking and collaborating with their neighbors about the problem. Kids should now be engrossed in a rotating combination of working on their own, talking with their neighbors about what they've uncovered, adjusting their strategies, and trying to solve the problem again. This will be a great opportunity to learn more about how students are thinking.

KIDS SHOULD NOW BE ENGROSSED IN A ROTATING COMBINATION OF WORKING ON THEIR OWN, TALKING WITH THEIR NEIGHBORS ABOUT WHAT THEY'VE UNCOVERED, ADJUSTING THEIR STRATEGIES, AND TRYING TO SOLVE THE PROBLEM AGAIN.

What Should We Do While Students Are Working?

In Chapter Three we spent time working on anticipating student responses, the first of Smith and Stein's five practices. As a result of that investment, we can now walk around the room and monitor students' progress instead of using precious minutes to solve the problem ourselves. While students will forever find new and interesting ways to solve problems or get stuck, we'll feel more confident during the lesson because we'll be familiar with much of their work.

It's at this point that the Student Strategy Tracker (Figure 3.2) we created in Chapter Three will come in handy. Whether we use it electronically or print it out and attach it to a clipboard, it will be helpful when keeping track of the ways students approach the problem. In the row for each strategy we can write down the names of students using that strategy. We might also want to jot down additional notes about their strategy as we might have many kids using each strategy. Anything that will be helpful later when selecting students to present their work will be worth keeping track of, such as notes about who explained their thinking well, used pictures, or labeled their units. For example, with the problem we've been discussing, some kids might end up with x having an integer solution while others might end up with x having a fraction solution. We might write this down in the notes if we prefer one type of solution when sharing.

We also want to remember our mathematical goal during this process so that we stay focused on which student work will best help us achieve it. In this case, our mathematical goal is helping students develop conceptual understanding of solving linear equations in one variable. So, while we're walking around the room, we'll focus on the next three of Smith, Hughes, Engle, and Stein's five practices: "monitoring students' work on and engagement with the task, selecting particular students to present their mathematical work, and sequencing the student responses to be displayed in a specific order" (2009, 550).

We'll watch students and listen to their conversations. We'll also want to be on the lookout for students getting stuck (hopefully in ways we anticipated) and use "just-in-time scaffolding" as needed (Dixon et al. 2019). For example, if students forget the procedures for solving linear equations, we should be ready to intervene. How we intervene will depend on how many students appear to have this problem. If it seems to be just one or two students with this issue, we can speak to them individually. If it's a small group, we can talk to them together.

However, if many students appear to have this problem, then we should call everyone back together and address the issue as a class.

Smith, Hughes, Engle, and Stein add that "monitoring involves more than just watching and listening to students. During this time, the teacher should also ask questions that will make students' thinking visible and help students clarify their thinking" (2009, 552). So, while we're filling in our Student Strategy Tracker, we should be actively thinking about which student work we'll select to be presented and nudging those students toward making their work as understandable as possible. We might help them solidify their thought process, have them label their work, write darker, draw a picture, or otherwise make it so the rest of the class will be able to follow their thinking.

Wearing our director's hat, we should be constantly thinking about the conversations that will help us best achieve our mathematical goal, including which students' work will get us there. While we could certainly change our mind, in Chapter Three we decided that beginning by selecting a student who guessed and checked many times would be ideal. The more times the student guessed and checked, the better, as all that work will more clearly show the strategy's inefficiencies. This example will set us up for highlighting the benefits of solving the problem using conceptual understanding, so we'll want to identify both a student who swapped coefficients and a student who swapped constants. Hopefully selecting these students' work and sequencing them to come after the student who used guessing and checking will help students appreciate a major benefit of using conceptual understanding: it often saves a lot of time and work.

WEARING OUR DIRECTOR'S HAT, WE SHOULD BE CONSTANTLY THINKING ABOUT THE CONVERSATIONS THAT WILL HELP US BEST ACHIEVE OUR MATHEMATICAL GOAL, INCLUDING WHICH STUDENTS' WORK WILL GET US THERE.

If we hadn't spent time ahead of class anticipating how students might solve the problem, we'd probably be spending precious class minutes solving it ourselves or trying to understand the many ways students could solve it. Perhaps we'd still be able to make the lesson work, but it would likely increase our stress level, decrease our ability to be thoughtful and intentional in the moment, and reduce the time we'd have available to support individual students or small groups.

Alternatively, we could just randomly call on students to share how they solved it. I've certainly done that many times. Unfortunately, what I've found is that this approach greatly reduces the likelihood of having powerful conversations. It's similar to taking the scenes of a movie and presenting them in a random order. While the resulting script might still be understandable, it's likely to be more confusing to viewers because it's harder to follow along and make connections. Sometimes when I've randomly called on students to present, it has felt like they were sharing scenes from entirely different movies!

It isn't my intention to say that there's no value to using these problems without having planned the discussion out. However, I have learned through trial and error that my classes consistently had more powerful conversations when I planned how I wanted the problem to unfold ahead of time by thinking about the strategies I wanted students to share and the order in which I wanted students to share them. Planning ahead allows us to spend class time actively working on making these conversations happen instead of solving the problem ourselves or figuring out why students are getting stuck.

What If Students Don't Use the Method We Had Hoped?

While we hope to anticipate the majority of ways that students might solve a problem, we'll still be regularly surprised by what actually happens during the lesson, so it's important to consider our options.

Sometimes the strategies we are hoping for won't emerge naturally. Other times, students will use a strategy that we had not considered.

With the problem we have chosen, we are hoping that some students will use a guess-and-check strategy while others will solve the problem conceptually. We need to consider the realistic possibility that the only strategy students will use is guess and check while the majority of the class struggles but never finds an answer. If this happens, we won't be able to have the conversation we had hoped for because there will be no students who solved the problem conceptually for us to call on.

In this situation, there are a few options. The most reliable option is to share work from a "student from last year" who coincidentally solved it just like we had hoped these students would. As you may suspect, initially the "student from last year" is me (or, better yet, a colleague with different handwriting). I regularly create student work samples for every Open Middle problem I use because it doesn't take much effort and it gives me a solid backup plan if I want to stick with the mathematical goal I had hoped for. Eventually, this premeditated work from the "student from last year" gets replaced with actual student work, which I scan and save. Generally, it's better to use actual student work from the class we're working with. However, in a pinch, we could have one of the students who used guess and check present first. Then we could present the work from the "student from last year" as something of a curiosity that the class can explore.

I recommend creating fake student work for every single strategy you might want to use, just in case. So for this problem, we should create work for a student who guessed and checked, a student who swapped coefficients, and a student who swapped constants. I have rarely needed to use more than one "student from last year" in a discussion, but it's a good idea to use different handwriting on each sample.

Another option happens while monitoring students as they work. If we're noticing that very few or no students are using the method we had hoped for, we can select one or two kids and give them more direct nudges. For example, we can say to a student, "I wonder what would happen if you used the same digits but changed where you used them." It might take her a little while, but if the student finds the second answer, we can follow up with, "I wonder if we can figure out why that worked." While this is not an ideal scenario, if we can get the student to make these discoveries, she will play a helpful role in the conversation that follows.

My least preferred option is switching the mathematical goal mid-lesson. Realistically, when most students are struggling and few students are solving the problem conceptually, it will make achieving our mathematical goal challenging. So, we could switch our mathematical goal to one that we do have the student work for, such as highlighting common mistakes so that students can stop making them. In general, this is a great backup mathematical goal, as there are often many student mistakes to choose from. While it may be disappointing if this happens because we won't have the conversation we had planned to have, switching mathematical goals will still be beneficial because students likely have misconceptions and missing foundational skills that we now have an opportunity to address. Addressing these issues will make future explorations that much easier.

So, in general, I like to have work from "students from last year" ready to go as a backup plan, which I replace with actual student work over time. Regardless of which option we choose, it's worth again acknowledging that we'll be much more prepared because we spent so much time anticipating potential student strategies and misconceptions.

Alternatively, if a student correctly solves the problem but uses a strategy we had not considered, we have lots of choices. First, we should always validate the student with a simple comment like, "This is fantastic! It never occurred to me that this problem could be solved using your method." This response takes very little effort from us but can dramatically improve the way that student sees herself as a mathematician. Depending on the mathematical goal we have, the student's strategy could fit in nicely. For example, if our mathematical goal is helping students use more advanced strategies, we can begin with commonly used strategies that we see from most students, then show less commonly used strategies, and finally end with the student's unanticipated strategy. Even if we stick with the same goal, we can still begin with a student who guessed and checked, then someone who used conceptual understanding (such as swapping constants or coefficients), and end with the student's unanticipated strategy.

What If Students Solve the Problem Using a Method We Don't Understand?

If we use Open Middle problems with our classes often enough, eventually a student will solve one using a method we don't understand. This situation has the potential to be anything from a complete disaster to a moment the student will cherish forever. Fortunately, we can skillfully choose which reaction to have, so let's discuss a plan for when this happens.

The most important thing to remember is that despite how uncomfortable this situation might make us feel, we want to validate the student and her work. Teachers will often say how they love it when students use unexpected strategies, but these moments can also cause anxiety. For example, we might not immediately know if the student solved the problem correctly or if she just made a series of mistakes and somehow landed on the correct answer. So, if a student shows us her work and explains how she solved it using a method we don't understand, the first words out of our mouths should be something like, "Wow. I've never seen anyone approach it this way." We aren't necessarily confirming whether her method is correct or not, but we are kindly opening the door to an exploration of her approach.

Next, we can ask the student a few follow-up questions and hope her responses will clarify things. Sometimes that conversation is enough, but not always. If we still don't understand how the student solved the problem, then we'll need to be very careful about our next moves. We have many options that range on a spectrum from awful to amazing. To get an awful one out of the way, we definitely don't want to say, "I wish you'd been paying attention in class and used one of the methods we've been discussing," which will create a lifelong unpleasant memory for the student. So, with that terrible response out of the way, let's explore more choices as we head toward our best options.

One option that sounds good at first but can be problematic is inviting the student to the front of the class to explain her method to her classmates. Initially this idea sounds great because it honors the student and her accomplishment. In reality, while there's a chance that having the student present her work before you understand it could work out, it often creates more issues than it solves. In the best-case scenario, the student explains her thinking so well that everyone understands what she did and values how she solved it. However, how likely is it that the method we didn't understand when she explained it to us will now make sense to the entire class when she explains it to them?

Additionally, as we talked about earlier, we want to be strategic with our storytelling, including what strategies we select and what order we sequence them in. Even if the student is able to explain her strategy so that the entire class understands, it might be better to have her share last, after the rest of the class has seen more familiar strategies and are ready for something unique. Instead, sharing it first could confuse the whole class and derail the entire lesson.

Accordingly, I do not recommend having the student come up to the front of the class to explain her strategy until we completely understand what she did, and we know in what order we want to share students' work. If she's right and we don't understand her work, it will be difficult for us to know what to say to make her thinking accessible to the rest of the class. Alternatively, if she accidently found a correct answer by using an incorrect strategy, the student could confuse everyone.

So, let's now talk about a few options I do recommend. The simplest one would be to follow up our first comment ("Wow. I've never seen anyone approach it this way.") with, "I'd love some more time to think about this." Again, we aren't confirming that her strategy is correct but are buying time to make sense of her work. What student wouldn't feel great about solving a problem using a method her teacher had never seen before but wanted more time to look at?

With that additional time, we could figure out what she did on our own later that day or talk to our colleagues and have them help us think it through. I've certainly called up colleagues to help me decipher student strategies. I remember specific times in both a third-grade classroom and a high school classroom where the student wound up being right, but I could not understand the method used until a colleague explained it to me. After such a conversation, we could then come back to her the next day and commend her for her great thinking and possibly have her share it with the class once we understand what she did and how we can help her classmates follow her thinking.

Alternatively, if we've got enough time during class but asking the student to keep explaining her strategy to us isn't going anywhere, we could ask her to explain the problem to her neighbor while we eavesdrop. For example, if we don't understand why the student chose certain digits, we could say, "Please explain to your neighbor how you chose those digits." Then, we could listen in and hopefully get clarification. This could continue for a couple more questions and even involve another student or two if needed. Listening to more varied conversation would give us more chances to understand how she solved the problem.

As you can see, there are many ways we can approach this, but they all share a common pattern. First, we have to validate the student's effort. Then, we have to make sure we understand what the student did before incorporating it into the classroom conversation. Handling this well can make a positive, lifelong memory about the time the student solved a problem using a method her teacher had never seen. Alternatively, handling it poorly could traumatize the student or confuse the class.

What Should We Do If Students Give Up After Trying the Problem a Couple of Times?

It's reasonable to wonder whether students will persevere long enough to complete a problem or instead get frustrated and give up. The honest answer is that initially, many students will probably get frustrated and give up. Remember that from their experiences, mathematics has been the class where their teacher told them what to do and then they practiced what they saw on dozens of similar problems. So, when they're given unfamiliar problems with no steps to follow and have to rely on their sense making and problem solving, they will feel a mixture of uncertainty and excitement. Fortunately for us, there is a tool we can use to make students feel much more comfortable through this process: the Open Middle worksheet.

Let's take a step back to understand why this worksheet is necessary. Traditionally, math students have been celebrated for completing problems as quickly as possible, using as little energy as possible. Think about the timed tests we completed as children, where our goal was to correctly answer as many problems as possible in a minute. Experiences like these have taught students that if they can't answer a problem quickly, they should skip it and move on. We have trained math students not to persevere, learn, and grow.

In humanities classes, where students have to write essays or reports, students don't expect to complete the assignment on their first try and instead see that each new draft builds upon their previous work until they've completed their writing. The process is not about each draft being perfect nor about completing the assignment as quickly as possible. As a result, students give themselves permission to improve each time. I wondered why we don't have something like that in mathematics. How could we help students realize that they could improve by trying problems multiple times and reflecting on their process?

This is where the Open Middle worksheet comes in handy. As Figure 4.1 shows, the front side has a space for the student's name, the date, and the period number as well as their first, second, and third attempts. The back side (see Figure 4.2) has spaces for their fourth, fifth, and sixth attempts. Each attempt has three components:

1. A space for students to solve the problem
2. A space for students to explain in words what they learned from that attempt and how their strategy will change on their next attempt
3. Places to record the student's scores for their attempt and for their explanation

The Open Middle worksheet normalizes the expectation that they're working on problems that may take as many as six (or more) attempts to complete. When I introduce and explain the worksheet to students, I explain that they can earn up to two points for each attempt and up to two points for each explanation. This incentivizes a subtle but important idea: While persevering through multiple attempts is great, students learn best when they take time to reflect on the mistakes they made and think about changes they'll try next. We do not want students to rush through their attempts, guessing and checking

Name: ______________________________ Period: ________ Date: ______________

First attempt: Points: ____/2 attempt ____/2 explanation

What did you learn from this attempt? How will your strategy change on your next attempt?

Second attempt: Points: ____/2 attempt ____/2 explanation

What did you learn from this attempt? How will your strategy change on your next attempt?

Third attempt: Points: ____/2 attempt ____/2 explanation

What did you learn from this attempt? How will your strategy change on your next attempt?

FIGURE 4.1

Open Middle Worksheet (front)

Fourth attempt: Points: ____/2 attempt ____/2 explanation

What did you learn from this attempt? How will your strategy change on your next attempt?

Fifth attempt: Points: ____/2 attempt ____/2 explanation

What did you learn from this attempt? How will your strategy change on your next attempt?

Sixth attempt: Points: ____/2 attempt ____/2 explanation

What did you learn from this attempt? How will your strategy change on your next attempt?

FIGURE 4.2

Open Middle Worksheet (back)

with no explanations about what they learned or thinking about how their strategy will change.

To emphasize this different approach to mathematics, when I first use this worksheet with students, I tell them, "I really hope you don't get the problem right on the first attempt. If you do, then you'll earn at most four points: two for the attempt and two points for the explanation. I really hope it takes you at least three attempts so you can earn more points."

Think about how we can change the incentives in math class by introducing this structure! Instead of rewarding students who quickly complete as many problems as possible, now we're rewarding students for a cycle of attempting problems, reflecting on what they learned from their previous attempts, and improving their strategy. These changes value growth and improvement over time. In contrast, consider what would happen if writing an essay or report were more like what traditionally took place in math class. Imagine that every time we started a new rough draft, we had to start from scratch and write it all over again. Now we would want to give up in that class too because it would feel like our previous work was a waste of time.

Using the Open Middle worksheet has led to my absolute favorite piece of student work, from an eighth-grade student I'll call Isabella. Figures 4.3 and 4.4 are replicas of her work on a fourth-grade Open Middle problem. Take a few minutes to solve the problem yourself before looking at her work:

> What is the greatest area you can make from a rectangle that has a perimeter of 24 units?

On her first attempt, she struggled so much that she couldn't even construct a rectangle with a perimeter of 24 units. Prior to using this worksheet, that might have been both the beginning and the end for her. Thankfully Isabella kept going.

Name: ______________________ Period: ________ Date: ______________

First attempt: Points: ____/2 attempt ____/2 explanation

8

6 6

8

area: 48

What did you learn from this attempt? How will your strategy change on your next attempt?

This attempt doesn't equal 24.

Second attempt: Points: ____/2 attempt ____/2 explanation

8

4 4

8

area: 32

What did you learn from this attempt? How will your strategy change on your next attempt?

The perimeter was 24, and the area was 32 but I think theres a bigger # strategy.

Third attempt: Points: ____/2 attempt ____/2 explanation

10

2 2

10

area: 20

What did you learn from this attempt? How will your strategy change on your next attempt?

I learned that the perimeter is 24 but theres a bigger area strategy.

Open Middle Worksheet - Version 1.2

FIGURE 4.3

Isabella's first three attempts

Fourth attempt: Points: ____/2 attempt ____/2 explanation

11

1 1

11

What did you learn from this attempt? How will your strategy change on your next attempt?

The perimeter is 24, but the area is 11 and attempt # 2 the area is 32

Strategy: use #'s with more than one row.

Fifth attempt: Points: ____/2 attempt ____/2 explanation

7

5 5

7

area: 35

What did you learn from this attempt? How will your strategy change on your next attempt?

Sixth attempt: Points: ____/2 attempt ____/2 explanation

6

6 6

6

What did you learn from this attempt? How will your strategy change on your next attempt?

Every time the width got bigger so did the

Open Middle Worksheet - Version 1.2

FIGURE 4.4

Isabella's next three attempts

On her second attempt, she created a 4 by 8 rectangle that had the correct perimeter of 24 units, but she believed that creating a rectangle with different side lengths might lead to a rectangle with an area greater than 32 square units. Again, realize that many students would end here, satisfied that they had a good enough answer. However, the Open Middle worksheet is set up to reward more attempts, so trying again to verify whether she was right would earn her more points.

In her third attempt, Isabella created a 2 by 10 rectangle. It seemed intuitive to her that multiplying by a larger side length should result in a greater area. However, when she saw that the area was only 20 square units, she realized that her previous rectangle had a greater area, so she kept trying.

As we can see in Figure 4.4, she continued on the back side of the Open Middle worksheet with her fourth attempt and pushed her strategy of increasing the side lengths yet again, creating a 1 by 11 rectangle with an area of 11 square units. As I walked around the classroom, I realized that many children were doing something very similar to this student. This is when my X-ray vision kicked in. In this moment I realized that these students had procedural understanding for how to find the area of a rectangle but little conceptual understanding. Specifically, they knew what numbers to multiply together but not why that worked.

I called everyone back together for a discussion and had two students come up to the board. I had one student draw a 1 by 11 rectangle and the other draw a 2 by 10 rectangle. Once the sides were labeled, I had them draw the 11 and 20 square units they contained, respectively. Many students did not conceptually understand the connection between the multiplication used to find a rectangle's area and its visual representation. I asked them to discuss in small groups how a 1-by-11 rectangle could have a longer side length but a lesser area. After much conversation, they realized that the area would increase if they had another row of squares rather than just an extra column. We can see that thinking in Isabella's comment of "Use #'s with more than one row." This was a conversation that would not have taken place without both an Open Middle problem to help me spot their misconceptions and the Open Middle worksheet, which encouraged students to attempt the problem multiple times and explain their thinking.

Now working again with increased conceptual understanding, Isabella switched toward making more "row[s]" for her fifth attempt and made a 5 by 7 rectangle with an area of 35 square units, which was greater than what she found in her second attempt. At this point she skipped explaining her strategy, which was not ideal, but we can almost feel her excitement as she realized that she could improve even more. She then tried a 6 by 6 rectangle for her sixth attempt and found the greatest possible area of 36 square units. She explained that "every time the width got bigger so did the [area.]"

The best moment came at the end of class when I had students reflect on the progress they made over their attempts. I remember this student beaming with pride as she realized that she solved a problem she might normally give up on. This genuine sense of accomplishment is something we hope students will feel during our lessons, so here are some thoughts to keep in mind when using an Open Middle worksheet.

I REMEMBER THIS STUDENT BEAMING WITH PRIDE AS SHE REALIZED THAT SHE SOLVED A PROBLEM SHE MIGHT NORMALLY GIVE UP ON.

Each worksheet is designed for a single Open Middle problem that will likely require multiple attempts. It is not intended to be used for multiple problems that each require a few attempts (for example, answering a different problem in each of the six attempts). As such, students could wind up using a lot of paper. So, once students have used the Open Middle worksheet a few times and are familiar with the format, they can start making their own worksheet replacement by doing a problem in their notebook, explaining what they learned and how their strategy will change on their next attempt, sectioning off that work, and then trying again.

We might also find that regardless of what we tell students, they will still feel embarrassed from making mistakes and erase their work, resulting in students whose entire work is just in the "First attempt" box. When we see this behavior, there are a few things we can do. We can have a conversation about what we value in math class and explain how we're more impressed by the students who struggle yet persevere and find the answer. We can demonstrate this value through our actions, such as highlighting students who kept at it, like Isabella. Over time, students will start to understand that they have nothing to be embarrassed about and that we value their growth. We can also have another conversation about how the problems are graded, so students understand that they are losing points by not showing each attempt. Finally, we might require students to use traditional pens for these types of problems, so that erasing their work is not an option.

If we don't want to grade an Open Middle worksheet, that's fine. I've come to realize that once students see that they can figure out how to solve these problems on their own, the points are far less important to them. Put another way, the points are an extrinsic motivator that become less of a priority as students grow their intrinsic motivation by developing self-confidence and a passion for problem solving. The points can serve as a temporary scaffold we can dismantle once students have developed the new habit of making multiple attempts.

There are two versions of the Open Middle worksheet: the student version (see Figures 4.1 and 4.2) and the document-camera version (see Figure 4.5). The student version has all six attempts on one double-sided sheet while the document-camera version projects better and has a single attempt on each sheet. You can download both versions of the Open Middle worksheet in English, French, and Spanish at www.openmiddle.com in the section labeled "Open Middle Worksheet," or scan the QR code.

First attempt: Points: ____/2 attempt ____/2 explanation

What did you learn from this attempt? How will your strategy change on your next attempt?

Open Middle Worksheet (Large) - Version 1.1

FIGURE 4.5

The Open Middle worksheet designed for projecting, with each attempt on its own sheet. (Only one attempt shown in this figure.)

How Can We Tell When Productive Struggle Becomes Unproductive Struggle?

We should always be on the lookout for when productive struggle starts to become unproductive struggle, as they can often look similar. For example, in the problem about solving linear equations in one variable, unproductive struggle might look like students repeatedly picking all four integers randomly and checking to see if their answer is correct. If students are truly picking their integers randomly, then noticing a pattern will be much harder and solving the problem will be a matter of luck.

What might look similar would be students who are doing a guess-and-check approach, but perhaps they're keeping three of the integers the same so they can see what happens when the fourth integer changes. This struggle will be a little more productive because the student will be learning how changes to a constant or coefficient affect the equation's solution.

We'll be more prepared to notice productive insights happening because we've worked on the problem ahead of time, made our own mistakes, and figured out how to find the correct answer. In fact, I have come to learn that if I do *not* get the problem wrong when working on it or cannot figure out multiple places students might get stuck, it's a very *bad* sign for how the lesson will go. Students will certainly get stuck, regardless of whether I know when and where it will happen. The more aware I am about where kids might get lost (because I also got lost there!), the more prepared I'll be and the better I'll be at genuinely empathizing with their struggles. It's our job to guide students through their struggles, so when their work starts becoming unproductive we can help get them back on track.

I HAVE COME TO LEARN THAT IF I DO *NOT* GET THE PROBLEM WRONG WHEN WORKING ON IT OR CANNOT FIGURE OUT MULTIPLE PLACES STUDENTS MIGHT GET STUCK, IT'S A VERY *BAD* SIGN FOR HOW THE LESSON WILL GO.

Whenever possible, I tell students that I also struggled with the problem they're working on. I've found that students love it when we tell them that we understand how hard a problem is because when we worked on the same problem, we got it wrong many times before we figured it out. It makes us more relatable, helps defeat the narrative that they're not good at math if they make a mistake, and shows them that struggle is a part of the process for everyone. So, we have to know what warning signs to look for, what we'll say, and what interventions to use.

For example, we expect that when students solve the problem we will give them, some might not remember how to solve a basic linear equation in one variable.

> Using the digits 1 to 9 at most one time each, place a digit in each box to create two equations: one where x has a positive value and one where x has a negative value. You may reuse all the digits for each equation.
>
> $$\square x + \square = \square x + \square$$

If we had not anticipated this hiccup, we might find ourselves walking around the classroom wondering why students were not making more progress. If we anticipate that this struggle is likely to happen, we should have our just-in-time intervention ready as a backup plan because it's likely that we'll need to use it at some point.

Sometimes our intervention might be as simple as asking students some prepared questions. For example, if students don't realize that they're incorrectly solving their equations, we can ask, "How can we check our work to figure out if we solved our equation correctly?" Often this question is enough to get kids to remember to plug their solution back into the equation. Other times, we'll need to have more involved interventions ready to help students remember how to solve equations.

How we apply this intervention will also change depending on how widespread the misconception is. Some classes won't need an intervention at all and we can just let them continue to work. With other classes, we'll have to pull some or all of the class together to get them back on track and productively struggling again.

To be clear, no matter how much time we spend anticipating where students might get stuck, they'll often find ways to get stuck that we did not see coming. However, the time we spent anticipating their struggles will still leave us much better prepared to step in and help them.

What Should We Do If Students Are Unproductively Struggling?

Using Open Middle problems will push students (and perhaps us) out of their comfort zone. These problems force students to think deeply about mathematics, and while we hope that they will persevere through the process, we may find them aimlessly guessing and checking or, worse, quitting. While this outcome is not ideal, we should be able to empathize with these feelings because we might have experienced similar emotions while working on Open Middle problems earlier (in Chapter Two).

When I first used these problems with students and they struggled unproductively, I was frustrated because I felt like they gave up too easily. With more experience, I realized that the bigger issue was that I was using problems they were not ready for. For perspective, even though I graduated with a bachelor of science in mathematics from UCLA (University of California, Los Angeles), there are many calculus Open Middle problems that I would now unproductively struggle with because it has been so long since I've thought about that content. In theory, I should be able to do these. In reality, I would look just like many students when working on a problem. I would guess and check for a while but quickly realize I had no idea what to do and give up.

So, when students struggle with these problems, we should empathize with what they're feeling and realize that, while they should be able to solve problems on grade-level standards, the reality is that there may be many gaps in their mathematical understandings that won't get filled overnight. I've learned that we need to be careful and realistic about the assumptions we make when deciding what students are ready for. What appears very approachable to us might seem overwhelmingly difficult to students. This often happens because we are so familiar with what we're teaching that it's hard to remember when we didn't understand our own content.

If this issue persists, it might be worth revisiting our earlier conversation (in Chapter Three called "How Should We Get Started?"). We discussed beginning with problems that are more approachable to help familiarize students with the types of thinking and struggle they'll find with Open Middle problems. This choice doesn't necessarily mean using problems from an earlier grade level. It could mean using a less challenging problem on the same standard (for example, Level 2 instead of Level 3), which would give students experience with grade-level content with an easier access point. If using a more approachable problem helps students productively struggle, that's a sign that the issue isn't their work ethic; rather, they were not ready for the problem we gave them.

Remember that when choosing Open Middle problems, it's often worth starting students off with something they can be successful with and then working their way up to more challenging problems. While this ramping-up may initially take more time, it will invite all our students into the mathematics, help us better determine what students know, and allow us to adjust our instruction before using more challenging problems.

REMEMBER THAT WHEN CHOOSING OPEN MIDDLE PROBLEMS, IT'S OFTEN WORTH STARTING STUDENTS OFF WITH SOMETHING THEY CAN BE SUCCESSFUL WITH AND THEN WORKING THEIR WAY UP TO MORE CHALLENGING PROBLEMS.

What Should We Do When Kids Get Stuck in Unexpected Ways?

I should probably tell you that I've used this problem once before with students. Just like we're doing now, I collaborated with a group of teachers to plan out the same problem we've been working on. Despite our best efforts at anticipating where students might get stuck, when we taught it to two classrooms of students, one group still managed to get stuck in a way we hadn't anticipated. I'll share that story now to illustrate what could again happen when we use this Open Middle problem with your students. As a reminder, here's the problem again:

> Using the digits 1 to 9 at most one time each, place a digit in each box to create two equations: one where x has a positive value and one where x has a negative value. You may reuse all the digits for each equation.
>
> $\square x + \square = \square x + \square$

When we were planning, we anticipated that students might get stuck using guess and check as their only strategy and not have conceptual understanding to fall back on. So, we planned a just-in-time intervention that we could use to gently help them think about conceptual ways to solve the linear equation. If they were stuck after they had found one solution of either sign, we would give them this nudge: "Find a solution with the opposite sign that uses the same digits." We hoped that this hint would encourage them to develop their conceptual understanding and realize that swapping constants or coefficients would give a solution of the other sign.

Unfortunately, that's not what happened. Instead, many swapped the entire expression on the left side of the equals sign with the entire expression on the right side of the equals sign and gave us something like $2x+3=4x+5$ and $4x+5=2x+3$, which we had not expected! Despite the time we spent planning and anticipating how students might correctly and incorrectly solve this problem, the possibility that students would swap the entire left and right sides of the equation never occurred to us. It made us feel all sorts of emotions, including shock (that this misconception still persisted), frustration (that after all our time spent planning, this still happened), relief (that at least we learned about this misconception while we could do something about it), and confusion (because we had not planned for this and were not sure about our next move).

These kinds of unanticipated moments are unavoidable. They're both the gift and the curse of using these problems. We want X-ray vision into what students know, but sometimes we'll find ourselves wishing we could take off the glasses and go back to the time when we didn't realize all the misconceptions they have.

I want to be clear that while sometimes we will know just what to say or do in the moment when students get stuck in ways we hadn't expected, there will be times when we will pray for the bell to ring and end class so we can have a few minutes to step back and strategize our next moves before we teach the lesson again. This still happens to me all the time. It can be very frustrating, especially when it feels like much of the needed intervention will address skills that students should have had before coming to your class.

TEACHING THIS WAY IS NOT EASY, BUT IT'S SOMETHING THAT HAS THE PROMISE OF HELPING STUDENTS DEVELOP CONCEPTUAL UNDERSTANDING AND BECOME DEEP THINKERS, NOT JUST ROBOTS WHO REPEAT THE PROCEDURES THEY'VE BEEN GIVEN.

So, when we were teaching this lesson and students swapped expressions on each side of the equation, we did feel overwhelmed. We had not prepared a just-in-time intervention for that misconception because we did not realize it was a possibility. While we did not have an ideal response, we decided to acknowledge that it happened, briefly explain why the two equations were equivalent, and move on with the lesson.

I'm not sharing this as an example of how we expertly helped every child understand. I'm sharing the reality that using Open Middle problems can lead to challenging moments that are not easy to handle. When these moments happen, we have to realize that they are not a reflection on us. Students had these misconceptions, regardless of what problem we used. However, we should give ourselves credit for trying to bring these issues to the surface, where we can address them. Teaching this way is not easy, but it's something that has the promise of helping students develop conceptual understanding and becoming deep thinkers, not just robots who repeat the procedures they've been given.

What Should We Do After Students Are Finished with the Problem?

When I first started using Open Middle problems, my ultimate goal was to have students correctly solve the problem. What I came to realize, though, with more time and experience, was that when students correctly solved the problem, it was not the end of the journey but rather a necessary stop along the way. Sure, it was great that students solved the problem, but what I was really after were the conversations and connections students made when they compared their work with other students' problem-solving approaches. These conversations helped students better understand their own work, broaden their skill set to incorporate their peers' strategies, and develop deeper conceptual understanding. So, once most students are finished with the problem, we'll begin our class discussion.

While students were working on the problem, we will have used our Student Strategy Tracker to take notes on which students were using which strategies. Now, as students wrap up the problem, we'll want to select the student work samples that will help us achieve our mathematical goal and put them in the best sequence for discussion. Figure 4.6 shows an example of a filled-in Student Strategy Tracker for this problem.

Strategy	Student Name(s) and Notes	Order
Guess and Check (Students randomly place digits in each box until they have both a positive and a negative solution, hopefully with many incorrect attempts.)	Lucita - fractions →Casen - integers (many attempts) many others	1
Swapping Constants (Students get their second equation by keeping the coefficients in the same place and swapping the location of the constants.)	→Dylan - guessed and checked at first but then swapped constants. Integer solution	3
Swapping Coefficients (Students get their second equation by keeping the constants in the same place and swapping the location of the coefficients.)	→Chloe - first swapped coefficients w/ the constants, then tried just coefficients. Integer solution Tyrell - fraction solution	2
Solving Linear Equation Errors (Students can't remember the procedures for solving a linear equation.)	Many	
Fraction or Integer Calculation Errors (Students make mistakes when performing operations on rational numbers.)	Jamie - fraction Juan - fraction	
Picked digits by reasoning about their differences	Ally - used digits that gave her a positive and negative integer solution.	

FIGURE 4.6

Student Strategy Tracker that has been filled in with student strategies

Hopefully, we can begin the conversation by having a student who used a guess-and-check strategy present his or her work. In situations like this, I look for a student who guessed and checked many times so that other students will appreciate that while the strategy worked, it was not particularly efficient. Figures 4.7 and 4.8 are an ideal example of what to look for. This student randomly selected numbers in each attempt, and by his fifth attempt found both a positive solution and a negative solution.

Next, we'll want to share work from a student who might have guessed and checked for the first equation but swapped either the coefficients or the constants for the second equation. Ideally, we want to pick someone who ended up with an integer solution so that students who struggle with fraction operations will be able to follow the thought process without getting lost in the calculations. Figure 4.9 is from a student who started by randomly choosing four digits that gave her a solution of −1. Then she tried swapping the coefficients and constants on each side of the equation. That still gave her a solution of −1, but on her third attempt she just swapped coefficients from her first attempt and got a solution of 1.

Finally, we could have a student who swapped constants share his or her work, like in Figure 4.10. This student randomly selected digits for his first two attempts, actually getting both a positive and a negative solution on his first two tries. However, he was curious as to what the pattern was and on his third attempt found that swapping constants also gave him a solution of the opposite sign.

I don't have a strong opinion as to whether it's better to sequence the student who swapped coefficients before the student who swapped constants or vice versa. Either way should be fine, but once we have a student present one of these methods, it might be nice to have the next student present the other method. Hopefully, having these students go after the student who guessed and checked will help the class appreciate how using conceptual understanding makes problem

Name: ______________________ Period: _________ Date: _____________

First attempt: Points: ____/2 attempt ____/2 explanation

$$2x + 3 = 4x + 5$$
$$-3 \qquad -3$$
$$2x = 4x + 2$$
$$-4x \quad -4x$$
$$-2x = 2$$

$$\frac{-2x}{-2} = \frac{2}{-2}$$
$$x = -1$$

What did you learn from this attempt? How will your strategy change on your next attempt?

I guessed these numbers.
I'll try four more bigger numbers.

Second attempt: Points: ____/2 attempt ____/2 explanation

$$4x + 5 = 6x + 7$$
$$-4x \qquad -4x$$
$$5 = 2x + 7$$
$$-7 \qquad -7$$
$$-2 = 2x$$

$$\frac{-2}{2} = \frac{2x}{2}$$
$$-1 = x$$

What did you learn from this attempt? How will your strategy change on your next attempt?

This gave me the same answer.
I'll try mixing up the numbers now.

Third attempt: Points: ____/2 attempt ____/2 explanation

$$5x + 7 = 8x + 9$$
$$-5x \qquad -5x$$
$$7 = 3x + 9$$
$$-9 \qquad -9$$
$$-2 = 3x$$

$$\frac{-2}{3} = \frac{3x}{3}$$
$$-\frac{2}{3} = x$$

What did you learn from this attempt? How will your strategy change on your next attempt?

I got a different answer. But it
was still negative. I'll mix them up now.

Open Middle Worksheet - Version 1.2

FIGURE 4.7

A student who guessed and checked many times (front)

Fourth attempt: Points: ____/2 attempt ____/2 explanation

$4x + 7 = 3x + 5$
$-7 \quad -7$
$4x = 3x - 2$
$-3x \quad -3x$
$x = -2$

What did you learn from this attempt? How will your strategy change on your next attempt?

This is still negative. I'll try changing just one number next.

Fifth attempt: Points: ____/2 attempt ____/2 explanation

$4x + 7 = 3x + 8$
$-7 \quad -7$
$4x = 3x + 1$
$-3x \quad -3x$
$x = 1$

What did you learn from this attempt? How will your strategy change on your next attempt? ✓

I got a positive solution.

Sixth attempt: Points: ____/2 attempt ____/2 explanation

What did you learn from this attempt? How will your strategy change on your next attempt?

Open Middle Worksheet - Version 1.2

FIGURE 4.8

A student who guessed and checked many times (back)

Name: ______________________ Period: ________ Date: ______________

First attempt: Points: ____/2 attempt ____/2 explanation

$2x + 3 = 4x + 5$
$-3 \quad -3$
$-2x = 2$
$\frac{-2x}{-2} = \frac{2}{-2}$
$x = -1$

What did you learn from this attempt? How will your strategy change on your next attempt?

From this attempt I learned that in this intance the numbers will be (-).

Second attempt: Points: ____/2 attempt ____/2 explanation

$3x + 2 = 5x + 4$
$-4 \quad -4$
$3x - 2 = 5x$
$-3x \quad -3x$
$-2 = 2x$
$-1 = x$

What did you learn from this attempt? How will your strategy change on your next attempt?

I learned that by making the number attached to the variable is larger than the other whole number will not make it positive either.

Third attempt: Points: ____/2 attempt ____/2 explanation

$4x + 3 = 2x + 5$
$-3 \quad -3$
$4x = 2x + 2$
$-2x \quad -2x$
$2x = 2$
$x = 1$

What did you learn from this attempt? How will your strategy change on your next attempt?

From this attempt I learned that the number attached to the variable directly relates to the answer, and that the variable that is subtracted from the other variable determines the end result. Once I find one I can find the other by simply switching the two coefficients

Open Middle Worksheet - Version 1.2

FIGURE 4.9

A student who swapped coefficients

Name: ____________________ Period: ________ Date: ____________

First attempt: Points: ____/2 attempt ____/2 explanation

$4x + 5 = 9x + 2$

$4x+5=9x+2$

$-4x\ -2\ \ -4x\ -2$

$\frac{3}{5}=\frac{5x}{5}$ $\quad \frac{3}{5}=x$

What did you learn from this attempt? How will your strategy change on your next attempt?

I learned that I needed to put numbers into the empty values to figure out what I needed to do next. Next I will use this strategy again and see if it works.

Second attempt: Points: ____/2 attempt ____/2 explanation

$1x + 2 = 3x + 4$

$x+2=3x+4$

$-x\ -4\ \ -x\ -4$

$\frac{-2}{2}=\frac{2x}{2}$ $\quad -1=x$

What did you learn from this attempt? How will your strategy change on your next attempt?

I learned that these two values on the left were less than the two on the right and the outcome was a ~~[illegible]~~ negative number. Next time I will see if I can put numbers in and ~~know~~ predict what I will get next.

Third attempt: Points: ____/2 attempt ____/2 explanation

$1x+4=3x+2$

$-x\ -2\ \ -x\ -2$

$\frac{2}{2}=\frac{2x}{2}$

$1=x$

What did you learn from this attempt? How will your strategy change on your next attempt?

I learned that the constant of 4 in the 2nd attempt was subtracted from both sides in that equation and the lower constant of 2 on the other side became negative. In the third attempt I learned that if I subtract a smaller constant from both sides the value will be positive. The next time I attempt this I will see if it holds true.

Open Middle Worksheet - Version 1.2

FIGURE 4.10

A student who swapped constants

solving more efficient. We'll want to check in with the students we've selected as they are finishing the problem to give them time to gather their thoughts and encourage them to make their work as readable as possible.

Sometimes we'll find that students solved the problems in ways we weren't expecting, like in Figure 4.11. In this case, the student used a strategy we had not anticipated. She did not guess and check, nor did she swap coefficients or constants. Instead she "picked these numbers so that on both sides there would be a positive number (when both sides are subtracted) so when divided there would be a positive number." Then she picked digits for her second equation so that "one side would end up negative." What's important to realize is that if we had not spent time anticipating how students might solve this problem, at a glance it might have looked like she'd just gotten lucky with picking digits. However, with more experience solving the problem ourselves and anticipating how students might solve it, we were able to see that she used her conceptual understanding to solve the problem in a way we had not expected.

We have many options when we get an unanticipated, amazing piece of work like this. We can stick to our preconceived plan, as that will still likely give us a great conversation. Alternatively, we can replace either the coefficient swapper or the constant swapper with the unanticipated work and make comparisons between the approaches. If time permits, we can have all four students present their strategies. Again, by spending time anticipating the many ways students might solve the problem, we'll be better prepared to be flexible during the actual lesson. There isn't one right way to do it, and we'll have to trust our instincts in these moments.

THERE ISN'T ONE RIGHT WAY TO DO IT, AND WE'LL HAVE TO TRUST OUR INSTINCTS IN THESE MOMENTS.

What we need to realize, though, is that if we teach lessons like these often enough, we'll eventually find that one day we won't get

Name: ______________________ Period: ________ Date: ____________

First attempt: Points: ____/2 attempt ____/2 explanation

$4x + 5 = 9x + 2$

$4x + 5 = 9x + 2$
$-4x - 2 \quad -4x - 2$
$3 = 5x$
$\frac{3}{5} = x$

What did you learn from this attempt? How will your strategy change on your next attempt?

I learned that I needed to put numbers into the empty values to figure out what I needed to do next. Next I will use this strategy again and see if it works.

Second attempt: Points: ____/2 attempt ____/2 explanation

$1x + 2 = 3x + 4$

$x + 2 = 3x + 4$
$-x - 4 \quad -x - 4$
$\frac{-2}{2} = \frac{2x}{2} \quad -1 = x$

What did you learn from this attempt? How will your strategy change on your next attempt?

I learned that these two values on the left were less than the two on the right and the outcome was a negative number. Next time I will see if I can put numbers in and predict what I will get next.

Third attempt: Points: ____/2 attempt ____/2 explanation

$1x + 4 = 3x + 2$
$-x - 2 \quad -x - 2$
$\frac{2}{2} = \frac{2x}{2}$
$1 = x$

What did you learn from this attempt? How will your strategy change on your next attempt?

I learned that the constant of 4 in the 2nd attempt was subtracted from both sides in that equation and the lower constant of 2 on the other side became negative. In the third attempt I learned that if I subtract a smaller constant from both sides the value will be positive. The next time I attempt this I will see if it holds true.

Open Middle Worksheet - Version 1.2

FIGURE 4.11

A student who used an unanticipated strategy

all the student work we were looking for. Sometimes we'll find that no students swapped constants, no students swapped coefficients, or even occasionally that no students guessed and checked. This is where it's critical to have work from a "student from last year." This work will give us a backup plan and allow us to have the powerful conversations we're working toward.

As an example of how this backup plan might work, imagine that almost all students guess and check while only one student swaps coefficients. In this case, we would have a student who guessed and checked go first. Next, we would have the one student who swapped coefficients present her work. Then, we could mention how last year we had a student who swapped constants and add that to the conversation. While this is not as ideal as having an actual student in front of us who solved the problem using this method, the backup plan will still allow us to have the conversations we need to achieve our mathematical goal. Then, once we find real student work, we can keep that to use as backup in the future.

How Do We Facilitate the Classroom Conversation?

With our students selected and ready to go, it will now be time to have the classroom conversation. To understand our role during the conversation, I want us to think of ourselves as the narrator in a children's movie. Without a narrator, children may watch a movie and enjoy the individual scenes, but they may not make the connections necessary to understand the overall message. The narrator's job is to help children make inferences and connect scenes, so they see how it all fits together. Similarly, our role during this conversation is to help students make connections between the big mathematical ideas.

As an example of what we don't want to do, imagine if we called on our selected students to come up and share their work, but we said nothing and asked no questions. As Elham Kazemi and Allison Hintz said in *Intentional Talk*, "math discussions aren't just about show-and-tell: stand up, sit down, clap, clap, clap" (2014, 1). While the class would hear all of the strategies, students might not understand how the ideas connected or realize how using conceptual understanding made problem solving so much more efficient. Instead, we can take an active role in helping students make connections, and we can strategically ask a few questions that may help students become better problem solvers.

So, we should spend time thinking about what we want students to realize about each strategy and what connections we want students to make between strategies. We also need to pay attention to how we form the questions and whom we expect to answer the question. For example, asking questions such as, "What answer did you get?" will lead to very short conversations that can be answered only by the student presenting. If we instead ask, "How did you get that answer?" we're more likely to hear the detailed explanation we're hoping for, but still only the student presenting can reply. If we change the question to, "How did she get that answer?" now we can ask the entire class, and everyone can participate in the conversation through turn-and-talks, small-group conversations, or large-group discussion. It doesn't mean that we should never ask a question that only the presenting student can answer, but rather that we should be aware of who our intended audience is and format our questions accordingly.

So, we'll want to spend some time thinking about what questions we might ask during the conversation, not to have a script but to be prepared to facilitate a rich discussion. When we're teaching the lesson and can't think of anything to say, we will be grateful that we

WE'LL WANT TO SPEND SOME TIME THINKING ABOUT WHAT QUESTIONS WE MIGHT ASK DURING THE CONVERSATION, NOT TO HAVE A SCRIPT BUT TO BE PREPARED TO FACILITATE A RICH DISCUSSION.

spent the time to create questions when planning. During the lesson we can choose which, if any, questions we want to ask, add questions we think of in the moment, or change the order in which we ask them.

First, we'll want the student who guessed and checked to present so that the class can see her actual work. We hope that students will realize that while her strategy was accessible, it was not efficient. We will have to be careful with what we say because while we want to emphasize that guessing and checking is not an ideal method, we do not want to make the student feel bad (more on this later). Another consideration is that when the first student presents, no other strategies will have been shared yet to compare her work with, so usually the first student receives the fewest questions.

Here are some questions we might ask:

- How did you find your first solution? (Ask the presenter this to help the class understand her strategy.)
- How did you find a solution of the opposite sign? (Ask the presenter this to help the class understand her strategy.)
- How did she decide which digits to use to find her second solution? (Ask the class this to make sure they understand her strategy.)

These questions are important because sometimes when a student presents her work, her classmates politely listen but are not really processing what they're seeing. So, this gives them a chance to make sense of what they saw and gives us an opportunity to walk around the room and confirm that students are noticing the right things.

Next, we'll call either the student who swapped constants or the student who swapped coefficients to share his work. We hope that students who guessed and checked will see how much more efficient these strategies are or that students who swapped constants will realize that they could have swapped coefficients (or vice versa). Here are some questions we might ask:

- How did you find your first solution? (Ask the presenter this to help the class understand his strategy.)
- How did you find a solution of the opposite sign? (Ask the presenter this to help the class understand his strategy.)
- How was he able to find a solution of the opposite sign so quickly? (Ask the entire class this to make sure they understand his strategy.)
- Why does swapping coefficients (or constants) give us a solution of the opposite sign? (Ask the entire class this to help build conceptual understanding.)
- How can we tell if this student's strategy will always give us a solution of the opposite sign? (Ask the entire class this to further build conceptual understanding.)

Finally, we'll call the other student who swapped coefficients or constants. We'll want to connect this student's work both to the guess-and-check approach (to show how this strategy is also more efficient) as well as to the other digit-swapping approach (to discuss how both could work). We might ask the following questions:

- How did you find your first solution? (Ask the presenter this to help the class understand her strategy.)
- How did you find a solution of the opposite sign? (Ask the presenter this to help the class understand her strategy.)
- How was she able to find a solution of the opposite sign so quickly? (Ask the entire class this to make sure they understand her strategy.)

- Why does swapping constants (or coefficients) give us a solution of the opposite sign? (Ask the entire class this to further build conceptual understanding.)
- How can we tell if this student's strategy will always give us a solution of the opposite sign? (Ask the entire class this to further build conceptual understanding.)
- Why do swapping coefficients and swapping constants both give us a solution of the opposite sign? (Ask the entire class this to further build conceptual understanding.)
- How can we tell if swapping a constant with a coefficient will always give us a solution of the opposite sign? (Ask the entire class this in case students think that it does not matter which digits are swapped.)

Here are some thoughts to consider about the conversation we're setting up. Each presenter will begin by responding to the same two initial questions. This opening will give the student a chance to shine and give the rest of the class an opportunity to understand the presenter's approach. During these two questions, the rest of the class should be listening, and some will be confused about what they see. So, after each presenter explains how she or he solved the problem, we should strategically ask questions intended for the entire class.

I recommend having students work in pairs or small groups of three to four when discussing the prompts. I often use a think–pair–share strategy and begin by asking everyone the question, giving them five seconds of quiet thinking time to get an idea of what they want to say, and then allowing them to discuss their findings with their partner or group. I don't have a set amount of time for this discussion and instead read their body language. When the conversations slow and students start looking distracted, I bring them back together.

During these group conversations, it's vital to walk around the room, listen to what students say, and formatively assess their understandings. Our X-ray vision will rarely have better clarity than in these moments because we'll get to hear what students know and what their misconceptions are. Sometimes we'll be thrilled, and we'll realize that students really do understand. Other times, it will be scary and will show us areas where students are confused. Either way, we'll use this opportunity to gather the information we need to adjust our instruction.

DURING THESE GROUP CONVERSATIONS, IT'S VITAL TO WALK AROUND THE ROOM, LISTEN TO WHAT STUDENTS SAY, AND FORMATIVELY ASSESS THEIR UNDERSTANDINGS.

After students discuss the question with each other, we should bring the class back together. If time is limited and we're confident everyone understands, we can move on to the next question or student presenter. Usually, though, we'll have heard something we want to address in the large group, such as, "I heard this group talking about how she found her second solution by swapping coefficients but that she could have swapped *any* two digits. Let's talk about that more to see if that's sometimes true, always true, or never true."

This response is just one idea about how to handle the information we gain. The point is that walking around and listening to students talk will provide clarity about what students know or don't know and will help us adjust our instruction to better meet their needs. We are strategically creating powerful conversations that will help students make new discoveries.

To be clear, it is not my intention to say that during the lesson we should ask only our prepared questions. We'll likely think of some great questions in the moment, and we should feel free to use those as well. What I've found is that teaching lessons can be stressful, and I sometimes forget what I want to say. So I feel grateful when I've written down questions as a backup plan so I have something I can read from with questions designed to encourage detailed conversations.

Furthermore, we can add any great questions we think of during the lesson to our notes so that we remember to ask them when we teach the lesson again.

What If Students Are Not Ready for a Conversation by the End of Class?

From time to time, students will not be ready to talk before class ends. Sometimes students are so confused by a problem that few have solved it, or sometimes there isn't enough time to spend on the problem before class is over. If students are too confused to have a conversation, we'll likely feel mixed emotions. We might feel frustrated because we were looking forward to the conversation we spent so much time planning, but we'll also feel grateful to more clearly see what kids understand and what their misconceptions are. Remember that we picked this problem because we thought students already understood how to solve linear equations in one variable and we wanted to be sure. So, no matter what happens, we'll have better information about where they are.

That being said, it's worth reflecting on what we can do to minimize the likelihood that students will be so perplexed by a problem that we won't be able to have a conversation. This confusion happens most often when students are working on one of their first Open Middle problems, especially if they weren't exposed to easier problems to familiarize themselves with the process. That's why I love doing more accessible problems like the ones we talked about earlier (Chapter Three, pp. 57–59) on the first days of school, as they provide a comfortable introduction to Open Middle problems by showing how math can be both challenging and fun.

Students also tend to be confused when I pick a problem on a topic I think they should understand, but they actually don't. To mitigate this issue, I've learned that regularly using Open Middle problems throughout the unit gives me a more accurate picture of what kids know so I can better choose appropriate problems.

Another reason students might not be ready to have a conversation by the end of class is if I didn't spend enough time on the first of the five practices for productive math discussions (Smith and Stein 2011): anticipation. The reality is that sometimes I don't have a lot of time to plan out a problem. In those cases, I might solve the problem using only one method. I'll have the answer, but I won't be as prepared as I could have been for all the ways kids might solve it or get stuck. As we talked about earlier, when I struggle with teaching a lesson, I can usually trace the cause back to being able to solve the problem only one way or not thinking of enough ways for how kids will get stuck (and what I'll do when that happens).

We should also acknowledge that sometimes there just isn't enough time in one class to have these conversations. The reality is that Open Middle problems don't always fit neatly into the time we're allocated to teach math. It might be because students took more time working on the problem than we anticipated, they were having interesting discussions along the way, or they had many misconceptions. In these cases, we can extend the lesson to wrap up the following day just like we do for other lessons we're unable to finish.

Sometimes, though, we don't have the time to extend a lesson. While this is not ideal, what's important to remember, regardless of why there isn't time for a conversation, is that having students work on Open Middle problems is still better than having them work on thirty of the same problems they already know how to solve. Regardless of whether we finish the conversation today, tomorrow, or not at all, students will develop deeper understandings and we'll gain valuable information we can use to adjust our instruction.

How Do We Avoid Hurting Students' Feelings?

Something crucial we need to consider are the unintended emotional consequences of the mathematical goal we pick and the students we select to share their work. For example, let's say that we consistently choose to begin with the most common strategy and move toward the least common strategy because our mathematical goal is for students to become stronger with other problem-solving methods so they can choose reasonable strategies for solving problems. This goal sounds commendable, but students might start to see our facilitation differently than we intended. Specifically, students might begin to see the first strategies as basic and ordinary and the last strategy as noteworthy and admirable. As a result, students might feel bad or get teased by others when they're called up first.

The same thing can happen when beginning with a less advanced strategy and moving toward a more advanced strategy. It also happens when beginning with a concrete method and moving toward an abstract method. Students might interpret the person who drew pictures as being less advanced than the person who used a formula. It can also happen when students come up to share mistakes, as people often feel uncomfortable being vulnerable around their peers.

All of these issues can be resolved, but we have to be aware that they exist so we can strategically address them. Bullies or class clowns who make fun of others cannot be tolerated, or authentic conversations will become nearly impossible. The most important thing we can do so students feel comfortable is create a classroom culture where students have a growth mindset, support one another on their journey, and celebrate mistakes. We can honor students for the varied "smartnesses" they bring to the math classroom and highlight students for demonstrating a range of mathematical practices, processes, and competencies (Horn 2012). We should also routinely switch up the mathematical goals we choose. If we always start with the least preferred and work toward the most preferred, this issue becomes more pronounced.

What Should We Do If Students Struggle to Explain Their Thinking?

Sometimes classroom conversations become frustrating when the rich discussions we hoped for are replaced by students blankly staring at one another. This is a common and solvable problem, but it's important to determine why it's happening so that we can implement the correct fixes. Reasons for lackluster conversations include the following:

- Students are not engaged in the problem-solving process.
- Students don't understand the mathematics they're working on.
- Students feel insecure and are concerned about other students making fun of them.
- Students think that only their answers matter, not how they solved the problem.
- Students focus primarily on the steps they took and not the reasoning behind those steps.
- Students talk at each other instead of listening to and responding to one another.

These situations have different fixes, so let's explore each of them to examine potential solutions. If students are not engaged in the problem-solving process or don't understand the mathematics they're working on, it's understandable that they aren't saying much. If I were asked to have a conversation about a topic I did not find engaging and didn't understand, I wouldn't say much either.

If students are not engaged, the first question I wonder is whether it's a *will* issue or a *skill* issue. If it's a will issue and students are not interested in what's going on, that can be a challenging problem to fix. The reality is that many will issues are complex and would exist when using another type of problem as well. If students have had negative experiences in previous math classes or were made to feel as if they didn't belong, especially because of their race, gender, sexual identity, disability, or language, it can take a long time to build trust, repair and forge relationships, and give students a true sense of belonging in the math classroom. Additionally, problems at home, bullying, or mental health issues would likely be better addressed by a team of people close to the student. That being said, I have heard many stories about students engaging with Open Middle problems after normally checking out with most other problems. It may take some time before students believe you are genuinely curious about their thinking and will treat their ideas with respect. So keep at it, as Open Middle problems combined with your patience and trust might reengage them over time.

If it's a skill issue and many students are missing the skills necessary to solve the problem, then having a classroom conversation about the problem may be premature. If this happens often, it's worth reflecting on where the breakdown happened. Was the problem too advanced for students? Were students getting stuck in places we had not anticipated? Were our just-in-time interventions insufficient? In general, I have found that when this problem happens, the cause is that I did not spend enough time anticipating how students might interact with the problem. I assumed that everyone would solve it like I planned, and when that didn't happen, I was insufficiently prepared. So if this happens often, we should spend more time anticipating how students might solve a problem or do the process with other educators who can bring additional strategies to the conversation.

If students are insecure and are concerned about others making fun of them, that is a classroom culture problem. We need to ensure that students feel safe enough to explain their reasoning, even if incorrect, without judgment from others. A single class clown can ruin a discussion if people feel afraid to share their thinking. Strong classroom norms need to be put in place and consistently enforced if we want students to comfortably share what they know.

If students are hesitant to talk because they think that only their answers matter and not their explanations, it could be because students have come to see math class as a race to get correct answers. How a student solved a problem can feel irrelevant on a multiple-choice test. So, the idea that teachers genuinely care about how a student solved a problem might be new for many kids and it might take time for them to accept this shift. One question I've found very helpful in realigning what kids value is, "Does anyone else have the same answer but a different way of explaining it?" That question emphasizes the process over the answer. As we show how impressed we are with the variety of methods used, students will start to realize that clearly explaining their reasoning has become the new status symbol.

Some students may be fully invested and giving their best effort, but they may be unsure about how their conversations should go. This phenomenon tends to look like students stating the actual steps they took ("First I subtracted five from both sides. Next I . . .") rather than the reasoning behind those steps. While this is something that should improve for students over time, one tool that may be effective is sentence frames. For example, we could place the following reminder on our wall or tape a copy to each student's table:

"First, I ______________ because I wanted to ____________________. Next, I ______________ because I wanted to ____________________. Then, I ____________________ because I wanted to. . ."

While not every student will need this structure, those that do will often find it useful in formulating their statements.

Finally, sometimes the problem is not that students don't know how to articulate themselves, but that small-group conversations instead look like a series of short monologues where each student states what they did while the other groupmates silently listen, awaiting their turns. No one responds to each other, and after each person shares their explanation, the conversation is over. When this happens, I often give students a small slip of paper with a list of choices for how to respond after someone explains their reasoning. Some of my favorite choices include "How do you know that?", "Why is that true?", and "Show me how that works." Clearly these responses don't work in every situation, but telling kids to reply to a student's explanation with a question like "How?" or "Why?" or a command such as *explain*, *draw*, *describe*, *show*, or *prove* encourages the speaker to further explain their reasoning. The end result is that students learn the basic interactions of a conversation, and occasionally it spurs authentic group interactions.

How Much Class Time Should This All Take?

Open Middle problems often take as much time as we give them, so it's important that we first solve the problem ourselves and think about how challenging it will be for our students. I could easily spend 20 to 50 minutes (or more) using a single Open Middle problem with students. I believe that the problem on solving linear equations we have planned could also take the same amount of time.

Sometimes I plan to use an Open Middle problem as a warm-up and then use other classwork later in the period. However, it's fairly common for students to get really into an Open Middle problem and want to continue working on it. I used to be conflicted when this happened because while I valued students' efforts, I didn't want to neglect the rest of the lesson I had planned. So, to make sense of our choices, let's consider what students will miss if they spend more time on an Open Middle problem. For me, it used to mean less time doing additional procedural practice from the textbook or worksheet. If that's what they'd miss out on, then I'd have no concern letting them continue to work on the Open Middle problem. If it's a different important experience, then our options include cutting the Open Middle problem off, continuing it the next day, or assigning it as homework to complete. Even if students don't find the optimal answer, all their work along the way will help them develop deeper understandings.

Some aspects of using Open Middle problems do take less time as students become more familiar with the process. For example, we'll eventually spend less time explaining things like putting a single digit in a box or not repeating digits (though not all Open Middle problems have these restrictions). We'll also spend less time motivating students to persevere, as they'll start to see problem solving as something they can do and want to do.

What Should We Do with the Information We Learn About What Students Know?

Open Middle problems can give us a startling level of clarity into students' misconceptions. We might find ourselves overwhelmed by the now obvious gaps in their understanding. What I've come to realize is that students may have misconceptions whether or not we're aware of them. So, while this information is not always pleasant to learn, at least being aware of it gives us a chance to do something about it.

In other words, these problems work great as formative assessments, not just summative assessments. I love the metaphor Bob Stake uses to clarify the two: "When the cook tastes the soup, that's formative; when the guests taste the soup, that's summative" (Scriven 1981, 72). It so clearly articulates that while both the cook and the guests taste the soup, they taste it for fundamentally different reasons. The cook tastes it early on so that she can adjust the ingredients. By the time the guests taste the soup, it's done and there's nothing else that the cook can do.

Like tasting the soup while cooking it, using these problems gives us information we can use to make adjustments before it's too late. It's for that reason that I recommend using Open Middle problems with students early in the learning process. Once students appear to have mastered traditional procedural problems, we should move them to Open Middle problems. The information we acquire will help us better adjust instruction to meet their needs.

For example, with the problem we've been working on, using it earlier in the unit will give us time to review and incorporate interventions to improve students' understandings of solving linear equations in one variable. Conversely, waiting until the end of the unit will still give us information about what students know, but that information may not be as useful because we'll soon be teaching something different and won't be able to incorporate interventions as seamlessly.

Now that we've spent time thinking about how to prepare to use Open Middle problems and how to use them with your students, let's talk about where we can get hundreds of free problems we can use with your students. In Chapter Five, I'll begin by explaining more about the Open Middle website, at www.openmiddle.com, where you can download ready-to-use problems. I'll then introduce you to a three-step process for creating your own problems or modifying existing ones.

REFLECTION QUESTIONS

Here are some questions for you to reflect on by yourself, with your colleagues, or on social media using the #OpenMiddleBook hashtag.

- Why do students traditionally give up in math class, and why might an Open Middle worksheet help students persevere through the problem-solving process?
- How would the time we spend anticipating how students might solve the problem help us better facilitate the lesson and reduce our stress level?
- How might the student work samples we choose, the order in which they're presented, and the questions we ask students affect how well we accomplish our mathematical goal?

CHAPTER FIVE
WHERE CAN I GET MORE OPEN MIDDLE PROBLEMS?

I hope you're excited to try these problems out with your own students, so let's talk about where you can get more of them. Your two best options are using problems that have already been shared on Open Middle or making your own problems.

Find Them on Open Middle

My initial recommendation would be to begin with problems that have already been made and are ready for you to use. By using problems that are ready to go, you can spend more time focusing on how to best facilitate the problems (like we discussed in Chapters Three and Four) and less time wondering whether the problems you're creating are any good. For example, when I first started creating problems, I rushed the process and sometimes made mistakes I was unaware of. To see what I mean, try the Open Middle problem below:

> Using the digits 1 to 9 at most one time each, place a digit in each box to make a true statement.
>
> $\square\square + \square\square = 31$

When I first used this problem, students started placing digits but then became confused and said it was too hard. I was disappointed that they were not persevering through the process, until a student called me over and showed me that it was impossible to make 31 using the available digits! Even if they placed the 1 and 2 in the tens places, the sum would already be at least 30 and they wouldn't have even done the ones places yet. Creating a problem required more planning than I initially expected.

Fortunately, there are hundreds of ready-made problems from kindergarten through calculus available online for free at Open Middle (www.openmiddle.com). You can browse the problems by grade level or search for specific problems by topic. I recommend you spend some time browsing the problems for your grade level to get a feel for the site.

On each problem's page, you will see the problem's name, the target standard, directions, any necessary images, hints (designed to give students a nudge in the right direction without spoiling the problem solving), solutions, the source of the problem, and the problem's Depth of Knowledge level. In the comments section, other educators share their experiences with using the problem, any additional answers they found, or modifications they made when using the problem. An increasing number of problems are also available in French and Spanish. Feel free to save the problem directions and images and add them to your classwork, homework, assessments, and presentations. I would not recommend having students go to Open Middle to use a problem directly off the website because they'll be able to see the answers and hints too easily.

If you've checked out Open Middle and still haven't found what you're looking for, or if you've now facilitated enough problems that you have a feel for them and would enjoy the challenge of making problems like the ones we've discussed in this book, let me share a three-step process for creating them. Remember, your ultimate goal is to create a problem that will allow you to facilitate rich conversations and spot hidden misconceptions. Many variations of the same problem might achieve this goal, so let's discuss the process.

Make Your Own Open Middle Problems

Making your first Open Middle problem can be a bit overwhelming because there are so many possibilities that you might not know where to begin. The reality is that there is no single correct way to make an Open Middle problem, and I'd like to show you what I mean. Let's experiment with modifying this two-step equation: $2x+5=-1$.

I've made seven variations of this problem using a process that was inspired by something Judy Larsen and Peter Liljedahl shared in their presentation "SmudgedMath: Blurring Tasks Sparks Mathematical Curiosity, Conversation, and Critique" (2018). All seven versions have the same instructions, so try solving them, and then consider each version's advantages and disadvantages.

> Using the integers -9 to 9 at most one time each, place an integer in each box to make two solutions: one that is positive and one that is negative. You may reuse all the integers for each solution.
>
> **Option 1** $\square x+5=-1$
>
> **Option 2** $2x+\square=-1$
>
> **Option 3** $2x+5=\square$
>
> **Option 4** $\square x+\square=-1$
>
> **Option 5** $\square x+5=\square$

Option 6 $2x+\square=\square$

Option 7 $\square x+\square=\square$

Option 1

$$\square x+5=-1$$

In the first option, students will have to think about how the coefficient affects x's value. In this case, when the coefficient is positive, then x will have a negative value, and when the coefficient is negative, then x will have a positive value. If students have conceptual understanding, this problem should be relatively easy. If not, there will probably be a lot of guessing and checking. Note that if the coefficient is 0, then the equation will become $5=-1$ and the solution will be undefined.

Option 2

$$2x+\square=-1$$

When the constant is missing, students will have to think about how the constant affects x's value. For example, will making the constant negative result in a negative solution? In this case, when the constant is less than -1, the solution will be positive. When the constant is greater than -1, the solution will be negative. When the constant is equal to -1, the solution will be 0.

Option 3

$$2x + 5 = \square$$

I would not be surprised if students thought that solving this problem was as simple as making the constant greater than zero for a positive solution and less than zero for a negative solution. Their basic thinking would be right, but the decision point for determining whether the solution would be positive or negative is five, not zero. So, making the constant greater than five will result in a positive solution and making it less than five will result in a negative solution. When the constant is equal to five, the solution will be zero.

Option 4

$$\square x + \square = -1$$

Option 4 now has two boxes to fill and gives students more to think about. For example, students have to think about how the coefficient and constant work together to affect *x*'s value. They might think that solving it is as simple as making both values positive or both negative, depending on whether a positive or negative solution is desired. It's more complicated than that, though, and depends both on the sign and the value of each element. This problem might even be beneficial to use after using Options 1, 2, and 3 as it builds upon the same conceptual understanding. One potential answer would be $3x + 5 = -1$ for the negative solution and $-3x + 5 = -1$ or $3x + -5 = -1$ for the positive solution.

Option 5

$$\square x + 5 = \square$$

Option 5 is fairly similar to Option 4 and again requires students to think about how the coefficients and constants work together. Students might again focus solely on the signs of the values they choose rather than the operations that follow. Option 5 is also similar to Option 3 in that the constant of 5 affects the decision point for determining whether the solution is positive or negative. One potential answer would be $-4x+5=-3$ for the positive solution and $4x+5=-3$ or $-4x+5=8$ for the negative solution.

Option 6

$$2x + \square = \square$$

Option 6 focuses on the relationship between the two constants in the equation. If students don't have conceptual understanding, they will likely do a lot of guessing and checking. However, if they do have conceptual understanding, they should realize that swapping any two integers will result in solutions with opposite values. For example, $2x+3=4$ results in a positive solution while swapping the 3 and the 4 to get $2x+4=3$ gives a negative solution.

Option 7

$$\square x + \square = \square$$

At a glance, Option 7 might look like the most challenging, but in some ways it is also the easiest. By removing all values, students with conceptual understanding will have the flexibility they need to quickly find the answer. For example, just like with Option 6, students can choose $2x+3=4$ and $2x+4=3$. However, if students have weak conceptual understanding, they could be guessing and checking for quite a long time.

I hope that after exploring these seven variations, you can see that interesting conversations could come from any one of them, and we haven't even talked about changing the integers students can use. For example, imagine using the same seven options but only allowing students to use positive integers. Modifications like these allow you to make variations of the same problem for different purposes, such as warm-ups, classwork, homework, and assessments. Let's keep this idea in mind as we proceed, knowing that there are many possibilities that will lead to deeper understanding.

Now, let's discuss a process for creating your own Open Middle problems. This technique is not the only way to create problems, but after using this method with thousands of educators, I've found it to be reliable. I am going to demonstrate this three-step process with three separate concepts in secondary mathematics (multiplying integers, evaluating exponents, and adding polynomials), with the hope that the examples will make the process clearer and inspire you to create your own problems. Once you've practiced these techniques, you'll feel more comfortable applying these strategies to more complicated problems.

Step 1: Start with a Level 1 Problem

The first step is choosing a traditional one-operation procedural problem. You can certainly choose more complicated problems later on, but let's begin with something simple for now. I suggest that you look for problems from your grade level with a single operation such as addition, subtraction, multiplication, division, exponents, or trigonometric functions. For example, you could choose multiplying integers, multiplying fractions, multiplying irrational numbers, multiplying polynomials, multiplying complex numbers, or multiplying logarithms. It generally doesn't matter what's being multiplied, subtracted, divided, or added. It just matters that there's only one operation. In the case of polynomials or complex numbers, they might contain their own operations (such as addition or subtraction signs), but we'll focus only on the operation connecting them.

You can usually find plenty of problems like these in your textbook, worksheets, or by searching for "____________ worksheet pdf" online. For example, searching for "multiplying integers worksheet pdf" will likely give you documents with plenty of examples to improve upon.

Multiplying integers

Let's start with something like $-7 \cdot 4$. We don't need to be concerned with the formatting, so -7×4 and $(-7)(4)$ are equally good choices. It would also work just as well to place the negative sign somewhere else, like with $7 \cdot -4$ or $-7 \cdot -4$.

Evaluating exponents

For this topic, we want a simple problem with an integer base and exponent, such as -4^5. As you'll see, at this point the actual choices for the base and the exponent don't matter as much as the structure of the problem.

Adding polynomials

There are an infinite number of variations to choose from with adding polynomials, so something like $(4x^2 - 3x + 1) + (-6x^2 + 5x)$ will work for these purposes. Other variations would work well too.

Step 2: Increase the Problem from Level 1 to Level 2

This step's purpose is to give us the first glimpses of X-ray vision, helping us spot hidden misconceptions and creating a context for rich conversations. I primarily like to accomplish this through two techniques:

- strategically removing some information from the problem, to prevent immediate calculations
- raising the quantity and kinds of solutions needed, to force students to think about patterns

Let's return to the three problems I shared as Level 1 problems and apply these techniques to them. Our goal is to increase the amount of thinking students need to figure them out by changing the problems so they are no longer primarily about computation. I usually begin to strategize about the choices I'll make by thinking about what misconceptions students often have with the topic. Then I think about how to craft problems so I can tell if students have those misconceptions. I'll think aloud through our three examples to show you what I mean.

Multiplying integers

From my experience, the most common issue students have with multiplying integers is knowing when the product should be positive or negative. So, when designing a problem, I'll try to figure out how to bring that concern to the surface. Here's a possible way to modify the Level 1 problem of -7×4 such that students will have to wrestle with signs:

> Using the integers -9 to 9 at most one time each, place an integer in each box to make two products: one where the product is positive and one where the product is negative. You may reuse all the integers for each product.
>
> $\square \cdot \square =$

My hope for this problem is that students will have to think about what integers to choose for the two boxes. For example, a correct answer might be $7 \cdot 4$ for the positive product and $-7 \cdot 4$ for the negative product. However, we might see students who do $7 \cdot 4$ for the positive product and incorrectly choose $-7 \cdot -4$ for the negative product. This response will give us X-ray vision into where students are confused and provide an opportunity to clarify this misconception. It's important to note that every student's first product will be either positive or negative, so asking for just one product won't tell us much. Asking for the second product will give us much more valuable information.

For example, if you see students guessing and checking to find the second product, it's a red flag that students are missing conceptual understanding. You might even consider giving students calculators to use, as those with conceptual understanding would find that using a calculator would slow them down. So, anyone using a calculator would give you additional X-ray vision because their actions would silently tell you that they had weak conceptual understanding.

I'd hope this modified problem would better highlight potential misconceptions including which students were confused about what happens when multiplying a positive by a positive, a positive by a negative, or a negative by a negative. Perhaps students will also choose integers with greater absolute values for the sign they want, like they might if it were an adding-integers problem. For example, some students might think that $7 \cdot -4$ equals 28 because the positive integer has a greater absolute value than the negative integer.

Realize that my choices could have gone differently and worked well too. For example, I could have put a negative sign before the first box, as shown below, or made both boxes negative. I could have also chosen between using the integers -9 to 9 or the digits 0 to 9. These minor adjustments would allow us to tweak problems to make new versions.

Evaluating exponents

After thinking about common misconceptions with exponents, I want to determine whether students understand how negatives work with the base or the exponent. Our Level 1 problem, -4^5, wouldn't push students to think conceptually or give us enough insight into students' thinking. Let's consider how opening up that problem to yield the problem below might bring these issues out.

> Using the integers −9 to 9 at most one time each, place an integer in each box to make two values: one that is positive and one that is negative. You may reuse all the integers each time.
>
> $\square^{\square} =$

Consider all the misconceptions that might come out from this problem. Students might put a negative integer in the exponent and think that will make the value negative (because they think they're supposed to multiply the base by the exponent), or they might put a negative integer in the base and an even exponent and think that it would be negative as well (because they don't understand how pairs of negative signs would undo each other).

Similar to the multiplying integers problem, any combination of integers will give the student a correct initial answer, as it will have either a positive or a negative value. Once they try to find an expression with the opposite value, the misconceptions become easier to spot. I'd again recommend giving students calculators because anyone who used one would be silently telling you that they had weak conceptual understanding. Note that this problem does not ask students to evaluate the expression and find the actual value. So, a student with conceptual understanding should be able to construct expressions with positive and negative values without finding the exact values.

For example, students could make any negative value from an expression with a negative base and an odd exponent. They could make any positive value from an expression with either a positive base and any exponent or from a negative base and an even exponent.

Adding polynomials

Some of the most common confusions and misconceptions around adding polynomials include not knowing which terms are like terms, not understanding what to do with coefficients and exponents, and not performing operations correctly. So, these are the potential concerns that I would hope to uncover with the Open Middle problem I created.

We started with the Level 1 problem $(4x^2 - 3x + 1) + (-6x^2 + 5x)$. I begin by removing all the coefficients, exponents, and constants and replacing them with boxes to give me a clean slate. This usually works, but if I find that the problem-solving process becomes too complicated, I can replace some of the boxes with strategically chosen digits. For now, let's begin with removing all the digits:

$$\left(\square x^{\square} - \square x + \square\right) + \left(\square x^{\square} + \square x\right)$$

Next, I try to think about what I might make students do to extend their thinking or see a pattern. What integers should I allow them to use: -9 to 9, 0 to 9, 1 to 9, or something else? What should their goal be? Asking them to simplify the expression and create positive and negative versions does not seem like a good fit for this kind of problem.

Ultimately, I decide that asking students to choose digits to craft polynomials so that their sums have more terms or fewer terms might help bring out potential misconceptions. Specifically, if I ask students to create two expressions, one with three or more terms and one with fewer than three terms, this may make it easier to reveal misconceptions we're concerned about. Do students understand what like terms are? Do they understand when you can combine like terms? Do they understand how the coefficients and exponents affect how the terms combine?

That thinking led me to this problem:

> Using the integers −9 to 9 at most one time each, place an integer in each box to make two expressions: one that has three or more terms and one that has fewer than three terms. You may reuse all the integers for each expression.
>
> $$\left(\square x^{\square} - \square x + \square\right) + \left(\square x^{\square} + \square x\right)$$

To complete this problem, students will have to understand how to choose coefficients, exponents, and a constant such that terms either combine or do not. Getting an expression that has three or more terms should be easier, as long as students avoid choosing exponents like zero or one and none of the terms add to zero. One example of an expression with three or more terms is $(4x^8 - 3x + 1) + (-6x^5 + -5x)$, which equals $4x^8 - 6x^5 - 8x + 1$.

To get an expression with fewer than three terms, students can choose exponents like zero and one that make other terms combine. One example of an expression with fewer than three terms is $(2x^1 - 6x + 4) + (-3x^0 + 5x)$, which equals $x + 1$.

My hope is that by using an Open Middle problem like this, many students who could answer a traditional adding-polynomials problem will have to think more deeply, make connections, and possibly show their hidden misconceptions.

Step 3: Increase the Problem from Level 2 to Level 3

Another level of rigor is introduced when you require students to *optimize* their problem solving, taking it from Level 2 to Level 3. This optimization might include asking students to

- make the greatest or least product, sum, difference, quotient, or answer or
- make an answer that is closest to a specific value.

I often optimize by modifying my previous Level 2 problem and asking students to find the greatest, least, or closest value. Sometimes this results in accidentally creating a trivially easy problem. While I'm always on the lookout for this possibility, optimizing usually introduces the need for strategic thinking. Guessing and checking might have worked well enough for the Level 1 and 2 problems, but it's usually a much less efficient strategy with a Level 3 problem.

When asked to optimize, students will often utilize their conceptual understanding and strategically think about the problem before they even begin to write. You might notice a student asking herself, "Where should I put the 9? If I put the 9 there, where will I put the 8?" Taking the time to think before making the first calculation often saves time in the long run and makes the problem easier to solve.

Let's revisit each of the three concepts we've been working with and consider how to ask students to optimize.

Multiplying integers

Our original Level 1 problem was $-7 \cdot 4$, which we modified to create this Level 2 problem:

> Using the integers -9 to 9 at most one time each, place an integer in each box to make two products: one where the product is positive

> and one where the product is negative. You may reuse all the integers for each product.
>
> $\square \cdot \square =$

To increase the challenge to Level 3, I initially created the problem below, which asked students to find the greatest possible product.

> Using the integers −9 to 9 at most one time each, place an integer in each box to make the greatest possible product.
>
> 

Unfortunately, this is now a much less challenging problem. Most students will quickly figure out that the answer is either $9 \cdot 8$, $8 \cdot 9$, $-9 \cdot -8$, or $-8 \cdot -9$. I could instead ask students to find the least possible product, but that would involve the same issue, as now students just have to make either the 9 or the 8 negative. Asking for the product to be closest to a number (such as −51) could be good, but it still doesn't feel like it brings out enough challenge or misconceptions because guessing and checking would still be an effective strategy.

So, for this concept, I propose a slight modification. Try the problem below and think about both what the correct answer is and what answer you think students are most likely to pick.

> Using the integers −9 to 9 at most one time each, place an integer in each box to make the greatest possible product.
>
> 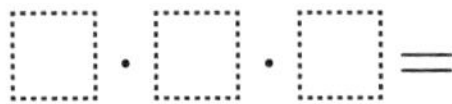

This problem is similar to the trivial problem, except that there are now three terms to multiply together instead of two. I believe that initially, many students will choose $9 \cdot 8 \cdot 7 = 504$ as their greatest possible product. This solution reveals good thinking, as those are the three positive numbers with the greatest values.

However, if students have conceptual understanding of negative numbers, they may realize that there is a greater possible product. Including the third box allows students to multiply a positive integer by two negative integers and still have a positive product. So, they may choose $9 \cdot -9 \cdot -8 = 648$, which is the greatest possible product.

I like this Open Middle problem much more than my initial version as it feels less trivial and has an optimal answer that would be challenging to find via a guess-and-check approach but easier to find by using conceptual understanding.

Evaluating exponents

We began with the Level 1 problem -4^5 and modified it to this Level 2 problem:

> Using the integers -9 to 9 at most one time each, place an integer in each box to make two values: one that is positive and one that is negative. You may reuse all the integers each time.
>
> $\square^{\square} =$

This was definitely an improvement on the original problem, but now I am trying to create a problem that makes guessing and checking a highly inefficient strategy so that students are forced to use their conceptual understanding. There are a variety of ways we could modify this problem, so let me first share an option I'm not a fan of and then some possibilities that could work well. I could modify the Level 2 problem like this:

> Using the integers −9 to 9 at most one time each, place an integer in each box to make the greatest possible value.
>
> $\square^{\square} =$

My concern with this version is that it quickly becomes a question of whether the answer is 8^9 or 9^8. This problem seems unlikely to force students to use their conceptual understanding or bring out the kinds of misconceptions I'm looking for. So, consider these three alternatives:

Alternative 1

> Using the integers −8 to 8 at most one time each, place an integer in each box to make the greatest possible value.
>
> $\square^{\square} =$

In this alternative, I modified only the integers students can use, which is a small change that creates a less obvious optimal answer. Some students might think that the answer is now either 8^7 or 7^8, but it is neither of those answers. Students can use their conceptual understanding to realize that the optimal answer is actually $(-8)^8$. Because I removed 9 and −9 as options, 8 became the best choice for the exponent, and because 8 is an even number, it allows students to use −8 as a base as there will now be pairs of negative numbers. Students might also think that $(8)^{-8}$ is an equivalent answer, leading to more opportunities to address misconceptions.

Alternative 2

Using the integers -9 to 9 at most one time each, place an integer in each box to make the least possible value.

$$\square^{\square} =$$

This alternative is interesting because asking for the least value forces students to use negative integers and consider where to use them. For example, you might expect students with misconceptions to use a negative integer in the exponent. They would find a fraction that was close to zero, but not the least possible value. Ultimately, they'd have to realize that $(-9)^9$ would give them the least possible value.

Alternative 3

Using the integers -9 to 9 at most one time each, place an integer in each box to make a value that is as close to zero as possible without being exactly 0.

$$\square^{\square} =$$

I also like this alternative because it forces students to use negative exponents, which they might otherwise want to avoid. You might expect students to begin with answers like -1^1, which is only one unit away from zero. That's a great first attempt, and without having conceptual understanding of negative exponents, that might be as close to zero as they'll get.

With conceptual understanding of negative exponents, they should realize that the exponent must be negative so that it can create an absolute value that is less than one. Then they have to determine that they want the absolute values of the base and exponent to be as great as possible. This thinking leads to an answer of 9^{-9}.

As you can see, each of the three alternatives might lead to valuable discoveries and conversations. When you're deciding which one you want to create, the real question to ask yourself is, "Which variation will lead to the conversations I am looking for?" Each brings out different misconceptions, and you could certainly use more than one of them with your students.

Adding polynomials

We began with the problem $(4x^2-3x+1)+(-6x^2+5x)$, which we modified to this Level 2 problem:

> Using the integers -9 to 9 at most one time each, place an integer in each box to make two expressions: one that has three or more terms and one that has fewer than three terms. You may reuse all the integers for each expression.
>
> $$\left(\square x^{\square}-\square x+\square\right)+\left(\square x^{\square}+\square x\right)$$

Next, we wanted to make guessing and checking so inefficient that before students began writing, they would stop and think strategically, considering the consequences of their choices. With this particular problem, I had to keep reminding myself about that goal, as it is easy to make a problem that is loosely related to the Level 2 version but doesn't assess the same knowledge. For example, I thought about making a problem like this:

> Using the integers -9 to 9 at most one time each, place an integer in each box so that when $x=2$, the result is the greatest possible value.

$$\left(\square x^{\square} - \square x + \square\right) + \left(\square x^{\square} + \square x\right)$$

I'm not saying that this wouldn't be a useful problem for a math class. However, because of the choices I've made, this feels more like an evaluating-expressions problem than an adding-polynomials problem. It would not give me X-ray vision nor lead to conversations around the topics I wanted students to know more about. Ultimately, I decided that if I asked them to choose integers to create a polynomial with the greatest or least number of terms, that would be more closely aligned with the standard I was working on.

Finding the greatest number of terms is fairly straightforward. However, finding the least number of terms is a bit trickier and requires students to become skilled manipulators of constants, coefficients, and exponents. So, this is what I went with:

> Using the integers -9 to 9 at most one time each, place an integer in each box to create a polynomial with the least amount of terms.
>
> $$\left(\square x^{\square} - \square x + \square\right) + \left(\square x^{\square} + \square x\right)$$

Again, students will have to choose values for their coefficients, exponents, and constant so that terms are additive inverses. For example, I chose $(4x^1 - 9x + 3) + (-3x^0 + 5x)$, which has a sum of 0.

As often happens, the process of creating these problems showed me gaps in my own understanding. Specifically, when I was done creating this problem, I wasn't sure if having a sum of zero meant that I had created an expression with one term or with zero terms. I asked my colleagues (https://robertkaplinsky.com/zeroterms), and I learned that this wasn't clear for them either.

This is the beauty and challenge of using Open Middle problems: they can show us areas where we and the math community are still learning and growing. When I was a child, I thought everything about mathematics had already been figured out. As an adult, I realize that there is still so much to learn and uncover. We can use Open Middle problems to help our students realize that they can contribute to this process while they are young and developing their own identities as mathematicians.

Make More Advanced Problems

As I mentioned earlier, when you first begin using these techniques, I recommend sticking to single-operation problems. Once you feel more comfortable creating Open Middle problems, you'll see that you can apply similar techniques to more complicated problems. As an example of what this might look like, let me share my own experiences with creating problems for the Pythagorean theorem.

My first step was finding a traditional Pythagorean theorem problem because oftentimes we can take a traditional problem as the foundation and make tweaks to it. Figure 5.1 shows a set of common problems.

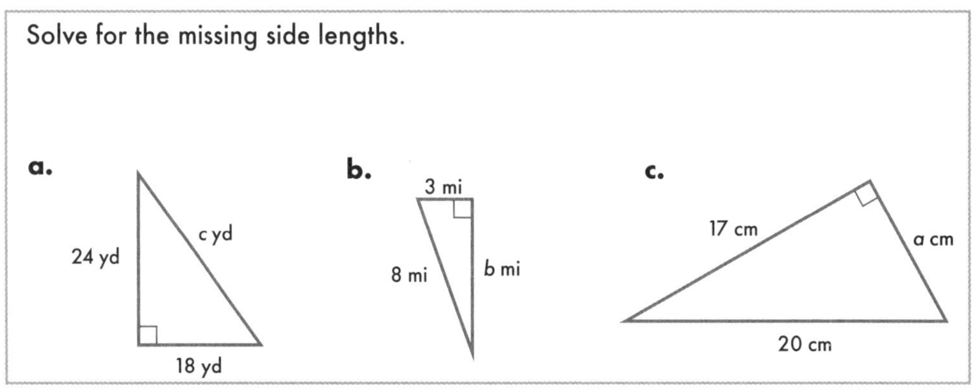

FIGURE 5.1

Common Pythagorean theorem problems

Any of these could work, so let's move forward with modifying Problem C. Next, I focused on how to raise the rigor and turn it into an Open Middle problem. I started thinking about what changes I could make. A traditional Pythagorean theorem problem gives two of the three side lengths for the triangle and asks the student to find the length of the third side. So, following the steps to go from Level 1 to Level 2, I thought about what would happen if I removed some information.

If all three side lengths were missing, I thought that there might be too much flexibility. Students could potentially just list Pythagorean triples. So, I thought it would be useful to define one side length and have students find the other two.

Next I had to decide which side length to provide and which two to leave for students to discover. At first, I thought about providing just the hypotenuse and making students find the two legs. However, I changed my mind when I realized that I could highlight a potential misconception if I chose differently. Specifically, if I defined one of the legs and left boxes for the other leg and the hypotenuse, I could imagine students finding two potential side lengths, but not realizing that the hypotenuse should always be the longest side. This misconception would be helpful to uncover.

I also realized that requiring single-digit side lengths would be too limiting for this problem, so the side lengths had to be at least two digits. I figured that three or more digits would require side lengths that were too painful to calculate, so two digits seemed ideal.

The next dilemma was what to do about the inevitable issue of irrational side lengths expressed with a square root symbol such as $\sqrt{7}$ or $\sqrt{34}$. I seemed to have two choices. I could let students choose where to place the square root symbol on either of the missing side lengths, which would allow more flexibility but could make the problems and instructions a little more confusing. Or I could pre-place the square root symbol over one of the missing side lengths. This would make the problem more straightforward but could potentially limit opportunities for creative problem solving. Ultimately, I decided to allow students to place the square root symbol where they wanted . . . at least at first. Try solving the version I initially created.

> Using the digits 0 to 9 at most one time each, and a single square root symbol, fill in the boxes to find two pairs of lengths for the missing sides. You may reuse all the digits each time.

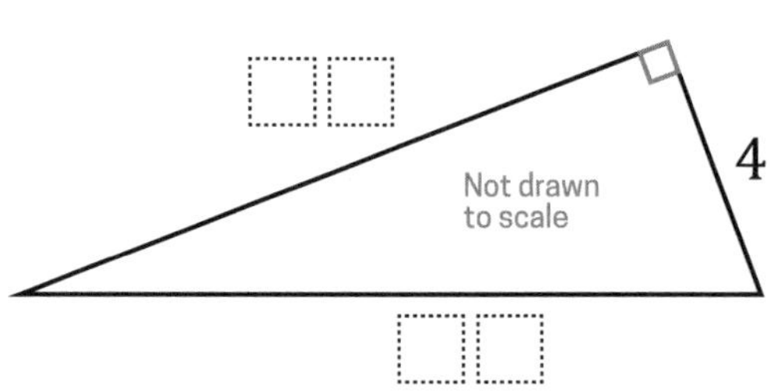

With this Level 2 problem done, I was most of the way toward Level 3. I now wanted to optimize the problem so that something had the greatest or least possible value or was close to a certain value. In this case, I thought it would be useful to make of one of the sides as long as possible.

My first thought was to require students to make the hypotenuse have the greatest possible length. Then I realized that if I required the leg to be as long as possible, it would be another chance to get a misconception to come out. Specifically, a right triangle's hypotenuse must always be the longest side, so if I required the missing leg to be as long as possible, it really should be the triangle's second-longest side length. I hoped this tweak would help my X-ray vision spot any remaining misconceptions that the Level 2 problem had not revealed.

To be clear, it isn't my intention to trick students. My hope is that if anyone still has misconceptions and doesn't realize that the hypotenuse always has to be the longest side, I want to know so I can intervene. That's why the information that this Open Middle problem provides is critical. Try solving the Level 3 version below.

> Using the digits 0 to 9 at most one time each and a single square root symbol, fill in the boxes to find the length of the missing sides so that the leg's length is as long as possible.
>
> 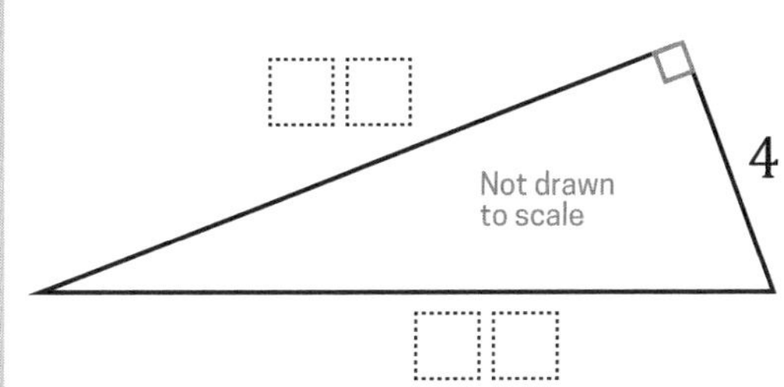
>

With the problems now in their first draft, the next thing we had to do was actually attempt to solve them. As we talked about in Chapters Three and Four, this step might seem unnecessary at first, but I've gotten into all sorts of trouble by skipping it. For example, I've made problems that had trivial solutions I had not considered or ways of solving them that never occurred to me. While these surprises aren't always bad, a problem that goes in a different direction than I anticipated can cause students to become confused or miss the mathematical goal I was hoping they would see. So, investing time in the problems you create is essential and worthwhile.

I was fortunate to be working on these problems during a planning day with some eighth-grade teachers in my district, so we worked on them together. For the Level 2 problem there were many correct answers, including 03 and $\sqrt{25}$, 05 and $\sqrt{41}$, and 06 and $\sqrt{52}$ for the remaining leg and hypotenuse, respectively. For the Level 3 problem,

I initially got a best answer of $\sqrt{65}$ for the longest leg and 09 for the hypotenuse. However, my friend and colleague Paul Chun found $\sqrt{84}$ for the longest leg and 10 for the hypotenuse, which was an even greater leg length.

Solving problems works best when done with others because sometimes we focus only on how we initially solved a problem and are less aware of how students might solve the problem. Working with more people gives us more perspectives. Solving problems and anticipating student strategies is a great use of educators' collaborative planning time.

SOLVING PROBLEMS AND ANTICIPATING STUDENT STRATEGIES IS A GREAT USE OF EDUCATORS' COLLABORATIVE PLANNING TIME.

As it turned out, neither Paul nor I actually got the optimal answer for the Level 3 problem, depending on how placing the square root symbol is interpreted. I only realized this later when I decided to share these problems on social media to get even more potential answers. Educator Farica Erwin tried the problem and cleverly decided to use the square root symbol in between the boxes. Using this strategy, she got $8\sqrt{6}$ for the longest leg and 20 for the hypotenuse, and I was so glad to realize that this was a possibility before using the problem with students.

Seeing what could be done with this problem was both exciting and humbling. The process also made us reflect on the choice to allow students to place the square root where they wanted. Ultimately, we thought that it might be too confusing for the eighth graders (and us!), so we revised the problem and decided to pre-place the square root symbol over the leg on both the Level 2 problem and the Level 3 problem. You could certainly make a different choice with your own students, but I share this experience to illustrate how there are many worthwhile ways to use these problems.

Here's what the revised problems now looked like:

Level 2

Using the digits 0 to 9 at most one time each, fill in the boxes to find two pairs of lengths for the missing sides. You may reuse all the digits each time.

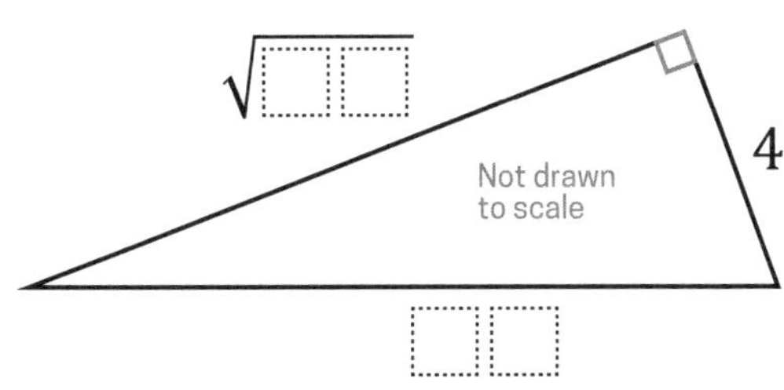

Level 3

Using the digits 0 to 9 at most one time each, fill in the boxes to find the length of the missing sides so that the missing leg's length is as long as possible.

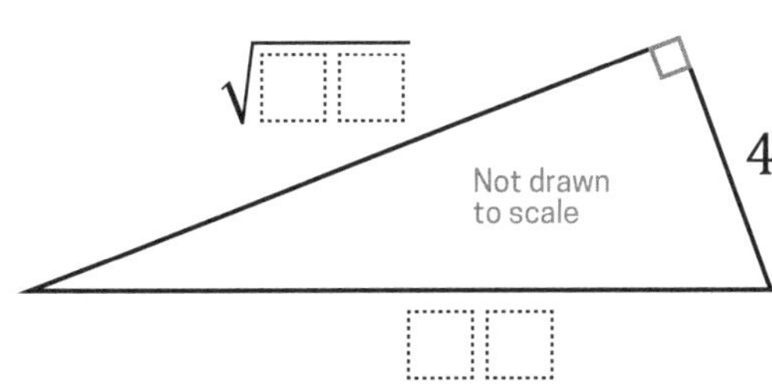

We hoped that these slightly modified problems would better lead students toward the conversations we wanted, and if they didn't, we could always change our minds by reverting them back to the original versions. At this point, we had spent a couple of hours on this process and were ready to be done. However, someone in our group asked about how many answers were possible for the revised Level 2 problem where the square root symbol was already placed. I said that there were probably many, many answers. I think I said fifty. Someone else thought it was closer to ten. Others were less sure. So we thought it would be a good idea to verify this.

Once we began, we realized that there were far fewer possibilities than I had expected. We noticed that the hypotenuse had to be an integer that was at least 5 because one leg length was given as 4. It also had to be less than 14 because the leg with the missing length had to be $\sqrt{98}$ or less (because it was the square root of a two-digit number) and the other leg was 4. This made it so the legs would not be long enough to form a triangle with a hypotenuse of 14 or greater. So, my supposed fifty possible answers were now down to at most nine!

We then worked to find what the corresponding leg lengths would be for those nine hypotenuses and got the following triangles (in leg, leg, hypotenuse order):

- $4, \sqrt{153}, 13$
- $4, \sqrt{128}, 12$
- $4, \sqrt{105}, 11$
- $4, \sqrt{84}, 10$
- $4, \sqrt{65}, 09$
- $4, \sqrt{48}, 08$
- $4, \sqrt{33}, 07$
- $4, \sqrt{20}, 06$
- $4, \sqrt{09}, 05$

As you may have noticed, many of these triangles break the rules of repeating digits or being more than a two-digit side length, so we had to narrow it down even further! Eventually we were left with only *two* possible triangles: $4, \sqrt{84}, 10$ and $4, \sqrt{65}, 09$. This realization also impacted the Level 3 problem, as there were only two possibilities to choose from. I share this narrowly avoided folly to give better perspective into potential issues that exist and the value of spending time actually doing the problems we make or use ahead of time.

A few days later, we tried the problems with students and it was a really rough experience. For better and worse, our X-ray vision glasses were blinding us with an overwhelming number of misconceptions, including these:

- Students viewed a square root as something other than a number. This was despite the fact we had taught them about square roots earlier in the year. They didn't understand that a square root represented the length of a triangle's side.
- Students did not understand the important balance between simplification and precision. For example, if they have $\sqrt{9}$, they should simplify it to 3 because while both $\sqrt{9}$ and 3 are equally precise, 3 is simpler. However, if they have $\sqrt{8}$, they should keep it as $\sqrt{8}$ because simplifying it to 2.8284... is not as precise. So, students did lots of approximations and rounding without realizing the impact.
- Students had gaps in their understandings of what a right triangle is. As an example, some students drew equilateral triangles (with or without a theoretical right angle) and assigned sides at random to be the legs or hypotenuse.

Some things did go as we anticipated. For example, students created impossible right triangles such as ones where a leg was longer than the hypotenuse or ones where legs were not long enough to connect to the hypotenuse (such as side lengths of 4, 7, and 12).

Overall, this lesson gave us significant information about students' understandings and misconceptions. We realized that we should have asked these problems earlier in the unit so that we would have had more time to do something about the results.

When writing, selecting, and assigning problems, we'll have to make choices and assumptions without knowing whether they are the correct ones to make. These decisions can feel uncomfortable. Realize that everyone feels this way, and this discomfort is part of the process. If we already knew how students would respond to the problem, we wouldn't need to use it. Thankfully, we can create problems that will give us high-quality information about what our students understand and where they are struggling.

Share Your Open Middle Problems with Other Math Educators

If you create an Open Middle problem that gives you X-ray vision, please consider sharing it with other math educators so we can use it too. Just go to www.openmiddle.com/submit/ and submit your problem using the form. We'll add it to Open Middle so that educators from around the world can use it with their students too. Imagine what it would be like if one teacher from every school district submitted one problem . . .

REFLECTION QUESTIONS

Here are some questions for you to reflect on by yourself, with your colleagues, or on social media using the #OpenMiddleBook hashtag.

- How can removing some of the information when going from Level 1 to Level 2 help bring out misconceptions?
- How can optimizing (asking for the greatest, least, or closest value) with Level 3 problems make students think deeply about the concepts they're working on?
- Why should we solve problems we create, and why would it be even better to solve them with other educators?

CHAPTER SIX
WHAT COMES NEXT?

I hope you've found the resources and strategies in this book to have huge potential for your students. If you're like me and other educators, though, you might be a bit apprehensive to use them. You might wonder how the lesson will go, whether students will persevere through the problem-solving process, or how you'll handle something unexpected. Thoughts like these cross my mind every time I use Open Middle problems too, and I'd like to share a story that helps me center myself when I feel this way.

In an interview with Guy Raz (2017), Jim Koch, the founder of the Sam Adams brewery, explained that while we may use the words *scary* and *dangerous* interchangeably, they don't mean the same thing. He goes on to compare rappelling down a cliff and walking on a snow-covered mountain on a warm, sunny day. Rappelling down a cliff might be very scary, but if you're properly using the correct equipment, it's not dangerous because the equipment is strong enough to hold a car. So rappelling is an example of something that is scary but not dangerous. Conversely, walking on a snow-covered mountain on a warm, sunny day is beautiful. It's not scary at all. However, these are the conditions that can lead to deadly avalanches because the heat can loosen the snow. So walking on a snow-covered mountain on a warm, sunny day is an example of something that is dangerous but not scary.

These differences between scary and dangerous describe how I've felt when thinking about incorporating new resources and strategies into my classroom. It's understandably scary to think about trying something new in our classrooms. However, are these resources and strategies dangerous for our students? Personally, I don't think so.

While few lessons go perfectly on our first attempts, using Open Middle problems with students will likely help them more than repeating the same steps over and over on a worksheet. These problems are about the journey, not the destination, so all the work students do along the way will help them grow.

Conversely, I remember thinking during my first years of teaching that if I could just teach the same grade level for a long enough time, I'd be set. I'd have all my lessons down, I'd know my standards inside and out, all my assessments would be made, and I could just coast for the rest of my career. That thought was not scary at all. It sounded amazing! However, with more experience, I realized that it was naive and dangerous for me to think that the skills I had when I first started teaching would have been enough for my entire career. I wouldn't have been doing what I should have to help students understand mathematics. Instead, the more I've learned, the more I've realized how much I still don't know.

As a somewhat tongue-in-cheek way to express the strange emotions this makes me feel, I often tell teachers that I'm embarrassed by how I used to teach, and I hope that they are too. The reality is that if I am embarrassed by how I used to teach, then that *must* mean I am better than I was. If I were still teaching the same way now that I was before, I probably would not feel embarrassed. So, while embarrassment is not always a comfortable emotion to feel, it's a great one to experience as a professional because it means that we've acquired new knowledge and skills that give us better perspective about what we hope for our students. As strange as it sounds, I hope I'm embarrassed by what I used to do as often as possible, and I hope the same for you.

If you're looking forward to using Open Middle problems and the strategies for implementing them with your students and colleagues, then you'll want to be strategic about what comes next. To help you think this process through, I've got a short activity for you to do. You can certainly do it by yourself, but it would be better to do it together with your friends and colleagues so that you can push each other's thinking because every school's situation is different.

Table 6.1 has five different actions (and two additional blank spots to add your own). In the four columns to the right of the actions are "Do Now," "Start Planning," "Yes and No," and "Don't Do." My recommendation is to fill in the table on your own, and then compare your completed table with those of your friends and colleagues. Your answers will be heavily influenced by where you and your team are in the process. For example, if you've just learned about Open Middle problems, you may be in a different place than someone whose school has been using them for years. As you'll see, the conversations you'll have about why you made your choices will be very enlightening. I'll share my own choices for each of the actions and my reasons for those choices in the following pages.

TABLE 6.1

Potential actions: How will you begin?

Action	Do Now	Start Planning	Yes and No	Don't Do
Incorporate Open Middle problems on assessments.				
Replace all traditional problems with Open Middle problems.				
Share Open Middle resources with colleagues to familiarize them with what's available.				
Find problems from Open Middle that we can integrate into our curriculum.				
Use the three-step process to strengthen existing problems.				

Actions to Consider

Incorporate Open Middle Problems on Assessments

☑ Start Planning

While incorporating Open Middle problems on assessments is useful because it gives you better X-ray vision into what students know, you should be very strategic about how you proceed. The first time I ever used an Open Middle problem with students was when I was working with a team of seventh-grade teachers to create a common assessment for 397 seventh graders.

The assessment measured students' understanding of the area and circumference of circles. They were used to problems like "Circle A has a radius of 10 units. What is its area?" and "Circle B has a radius of 10 units. What is its circumference?" We wanted to see how deep their understanding was, so we came up with the problem "Which circle is bigger: one with an area of 30 square units or one with a circumference of 30 units? How do you know?" This Level 2 problem seemed fairly similar to the problems students were already working with, so we figured, "How hard could this be?" You may already see where this story is headed. We did not.

When we looked at the assessment results, we saw that around 70 percent to 80 percent of students correctly answered the two traditional questions about the area and circumference of circles. However, only about 12 percent of students got full credit on the Open Middle problem! That day, we learned that we probably shouldn't assess students at deeper levels of understanding if we've never even exposed them to similar problems during class. So, I recommend that educators start by using Open Middle problems in their classrooms and start planning how to eventually use them on assessments.

Replace All Traditional Problems with Open Middle Problems

☑ Don't Do

If you're thinking that Open Middle problems are amazing and you want every child to solve them, I totally agree with you. However, completely eliminating all traditional problems is probably not something you'll want to do. Traditional problems serve a purpose and are useful for quickly identifying basic understandings. To be clear, while I'm recommending that you do not remove them entirely, I also recommend that we don't give students dozens of these problems either. Simply put, once it is clear that students understand how to do a traditional Level 1 problem, I suggest moving on to a more challenging Open Middle problem at Level 2 or 3 on the same standard.

Share Open Middle Resources with Colleagues to Familiarize Them with What's Available

☑ Do Now

The rule of seven in marketing states that a person needs to be exposed to a message at least seven times before she or he will act. So, while you may be ready to immediately implement these ideas, it could take others some time to warm up to them. I'd recommend beginning by sharing resources like my Depth of Knowledge (DOK) matrices, which you can download for free from my website (https://robertkaplinsky.com/tag/dok-matrix/). There are separate printable matrices for elementary and secondary grades as well as a combined elementary and secondary matrix. Figures 6.1 and 6.2 show the front and back sides of the secondary matrix.

Each matrix takes a single mathematics standard and lists examples of what that standard would look like as a DOK 1, DOK 2, and DOK 3 (or Level 1, 2, and 3) problem. You can think of it as an easily sharable version of the problems you saw in Chapter Two. The answers to the Level 2 and 3 problems on the matrices are on the Open Middle

FIGURE 6.1

Secondary matrix (front) showing middle school problems

Depth of Knowledge Matrix - Secondary Math

Topic	Dividing Fractions	Solving Two-Step Equations	Exponents	Solving Equations with Variables on Both Sides
CCSS Standard(s)	• 6.NS.1	• 7.EE.4a	• 8.EE.1	• 8.EE.8 • A-REI.3
DOK 1 Example	Evaluate. $\frac{4}{9} \div \frac{2}{5}$	Solve for x. $2x + 3 = 9$	Evaluate. 3^4	Solve for x. $3x + 2 = -2x + 4$
DOK 2 Example	Using the digits 1 to 9 at most one time each, fill in the boxes to make two different pairs of fractions that have a quotient of 2/3. $\frac{\square}{\square} \div \frac{\square}{\square} = \frac{2}{3}$	Using the digits 1 to 9 at most one time each, fill in the boxes to create two equations: one where x has a positive value and one where x has a negative value. $\square x + \square = \square$	Using the digits 1 to 9 at most one time each, fill in the boxes to make two true number sentences. $\square^{\square} = 64$	Using the digits 1 to 9 at most *two* times each, fill in the boxes to make an equation with no solutions. $\square x + \square = \square x + \square$
DOK 3 Example	Using the digits 1 to 9 at most one time each, fill in the boxes to make two fractions that have a quotient that is as close to 4/11 as possible. $\frac{\square}{\square} \div \frac{\square}{\square}$	Using the digits 1 to 9 at most one time each, fill in the boxes to create an equation where x has the greatest possible value. $\square x + \square = \square$	Using the digits 1 to 9 at most one time each, fill in the boxes to make a result that has the greatest value possible. $\square^{\square} = \square\square\square$	Using the digits 1 to 9 at most one time each, fill in the boxes so that the solution is closest to zero. $\square x + \square = \square x + \square$

Robert Kaplinsky

More free DOK 2 & 3 problems available at openmiddle.com

Version 1.8

FIGURE 6.2

Secondary matrix (back) showing high school problems

Depth of Knowledge Matrix - Secondary Math

Topic	Geometric Proofs	Complex Numbers	Trigonometric Functions	Definite Integrals
CCSS Standard(s)	• G-CO.11	• N-CN.2	• F-TF.3	• N/A
DOK 1 Example	Add one geometric marking to demonstrate the quadrilateral is a square.	Multiply the binomials. $(3+4i)(2+3i)$	Evaluate. $\sin\frac{\pi}{3}$	Solve. $\int_2^6 x^3\,dx$
DOK 2 Example	Use exactly five geometric markings to show that a quadrilateral is a square.	Using the integers -9 to 9 at most one time each, fill in the boxes twice: once to make a positive real number product and once to make a negative real number product. $(\square+\square i)(\square+\square i)$	Using the digits 1 to 9 at most one time each, fill in the boxes to make two true number sentences. $\sin\frac{\square\pi}{\square}=1$	Using the digits 1 to 9 at most one time each, fill in the boxes to make a positive and a negative solution. $\int_{\square}^{\square} x^{\square}\,dx$
DOK 3 Example	What is the least number of geometric markings needed to demonstrate that a quadrilateral is a square?	Using the integers -9 to 9 at most one time each, fill in the boxes to make a real number product with the greatest value. $(\square+\square i)(\square+\square i)$	Using the digits 1 to 9 at most one time each, fill in the boxes to find the function's greatest possible value. $\sin\frac{\square\pi}{\square}=\frac{\sqrt{\square}}{\square}$	Using the digits 1 to 9 at most one time each, fill in the boxes to make a solution that is as close to 100 as possible. $\int_{\square}^{\square} x^{\square}\,dx$

Robert Kaplinsky

More free DOK 2 & 3 problems available at openmiddle.com

Version 1.8

website. Sharing these matrices and other Open Middle problems at their grade level will help your colleagues gradually become more aware and receptive to learning more.

Find Problems from Open Middle That We Can Integrate into Our Curriculum

☑ Do Now

As I talked about in Chapter Five, there are hundreds of ready-to-use problems on the Open Middle website (www.openmiddle.com) that come with hints, answers, and often comments and suggestions from other educators who have used them. Using these problems is a great way to gain experience with Open Middle problems and how students will respond. They also save you valuable time, which you can use to prepare for the problem, including anticipating how students might solve it.

Use the Three-Step Process to Strengthen Existing Problems

☑ Yes and No

While there are many problems on the Open Middle website, you might eventually find a standard with no problems. So, it is *yes* because at that point, you have a process you could use to make your own Open Middle problems. However, it is also *no* because it's a good idea to check the Open Middle website to see if a problem already exists because you can save yourself valuable time and will often love what another educator has created.

Final Thoughts

I want to share one final story from Wendy Kozina, a seventh- and eighth-grade teacher from Bainbridge Island, Washington, whose students were working on the problem below.

Using the integers 1 to 20 at most one time each, fill in the boxes to create an equivalent expression.

$$\left(2^{\square}\right)^{\square} = \frac{\left(2^{\square}\right)^{\square}}{\left(2^{\square}\right)^{\square}} = 2^{\square} \cdot 2^{\square} = \frac{2^{\square}}{2^{\square}}$$

She went on social media on a Friday to share the photographs in Figures 6.3 and 6.4 and said:

> Kids begging for more time and yelling 'No' when I asked if they wanted a hint. Amazing activity. It made my day . . . I had kids asking me to take a picture of their work because they "worked all class period and finally got it."

She then followed that up on Monday by sharing,

> They are still coming in! Student shows up before school Monday morning and says, "I need to finish that problem we did in class on Friday! I was thinking about it all weekend!" She did it and high fives all around!

Open Middle problems present an opportunity to change how students, parents, and teachers see mathematics. I hope you're excited about using them with your students and that the strategies we've discussed have helped you feel prepared for success. These problems will give you X-ray vision and enable you to spot students' struggles so that it will be easier to help them while there's still time. Complaints from

FIGURE 6.3

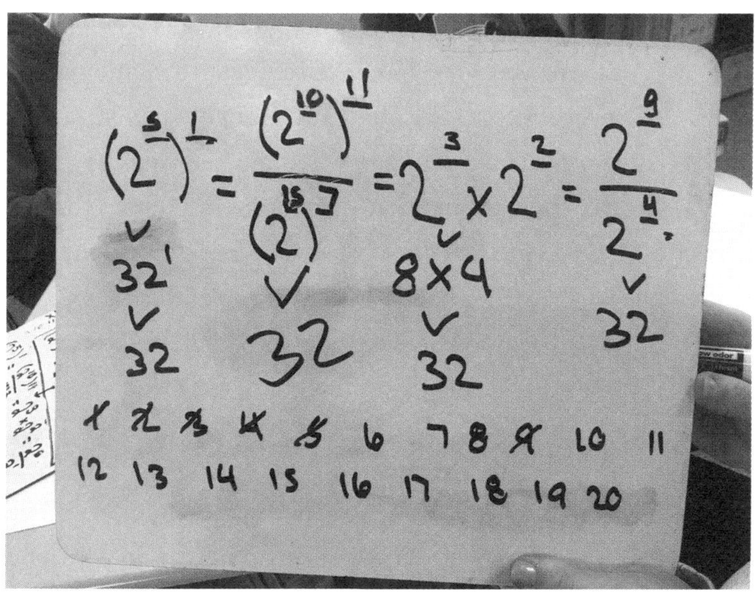

Student proudly sharing her progress

FIGURE 6.4

Students working through the problem

parents of students claiming to be bored in math class will fade away as we use Open Middle problems to challenge students with grade-level content. Get ready for a laugh when students don't want to stop working on a problem when the bell rings or grumble when you don't give them Open Middle problems as often as they'd like. It's going to be a wild ride and I'm excited for what's ahead for you and your students.

Now that you've read the book, there are a couple more things I'd love for you to do. First, download the resources I've mentioned in the book, including the following:

- the Open Middle worksheets in English, French, or Spanish
- matrices that show Open Middle problems at Levels 1, 2, and 3 for both elementary and secondary standards
- links to hundreds more Open Middle problems

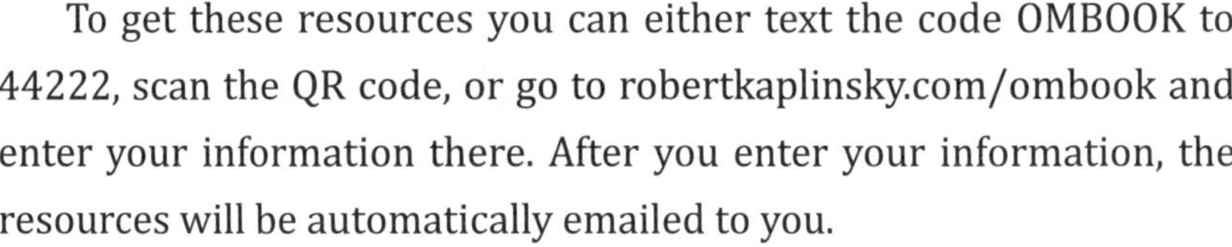

To get these resources you can either text the code OMBOOK to 44222, scan the QR code, or go to robertkaplinsky.com/ombook and enter your information there. After you enter your information, the resources will be automatically emailed to you.

Then, reach out to me on social media using @robertkaplinsky and the hashtag #OpenMiddleBook. I'd love to read about your experiences with this book or with using Open Middle problems, including what resonated with you, other answers you found, your successes, and any aha moments you had.

Thank you.

Robert

REFERENCES

Cook, Marcy. n.d. Marcy Cook Math. www.marcycookmath.com.

Dixon, Juli K., Lisa A. Brooks, and Melissa R. Carli. 2019. *Making Sense of Mathematics for Teaching the Small Group*. Bloomington, IN: Solution Tree.

Eisenhower, Dwight. 1962. *Six Crises*. New York: Doubleday.

Horn, Ilana Seidel. 2012. *Strength in Numbers: Collaborative Learning in Secondary Mathematics.* Reston, VA: National Council of Teachers of Mathematics.

Kazemi, Elham, and Allison Hintz. 2014. *Intentional Talk: How to Structure and Lead Productive Mathematical Discussions*. Portland, ME: Stenhouse.

Larsen, Judy, and Peter Liljedahl, and Norma Gordon. 2018. "SmudgedMath: Blurring Tasks Sparks Mathematical Curiosity, Conversation, and Critique." Presented November 18 at NCTM Regional Conference, Seattle, WA.

Meyer, Dan. 2014. "Video Games and Making Math More Like Things Students Like." *Dy/Dan* (blog), December 16. blog.mrmeyer.com/2014/video-games-making-math-more-like-things-students-like.

———. 2015. "If Math Is the Aspirin, Then How Do You Create the Headache?" *Dy/Dan* (blog), June 17. blog.mrmeyer.com/2015/if-math-is-the-aspirin-then-how-do-you-create-the-headache.

Raz, Guy. 2017. "Samuel Adams: Jim Koch." *How I Built This with Guy Raz*, July 23. www.stitcher.com/podcast/national-public-radio/how-i-built-this/e/samuel-adams-jim-koch-48094048.

Scriven, Michael. 1981. *Evaluation Thesaurus*. Inverness, CA: Edgepress.

Searle, John. 1980. "Minds, Brains and Programs." *Behavioral and Brain Sciences* 3 (3): 417–57.

Small, Marian. 2009. *Good Questions: Great Ways to Differentiate Mathematics Instruction*. New York: Teachers College Press.

Smith, Margaret S., Elizabeth K. Hughes, Randi A. Engle, and Mary Kay Stein. 2009. "Orchestrating Discussions." *Mathematics Teaching in the Middle School* 14 (9): 548–56.

Smith, Margaret S., and Mary Kay Stein. 2011. *Five Practices for Orchestrating Productive Mathematics Discussions*. Thousand Oaks, CA: Corwin.

Webb, Norman. 1997. *Criteria for Alignment of Expectations and Assessments in Mathematics and Science Education*. Research monograph no. 6. Madison, WI: National Institute for Science Education and Washington, DC: Council of Chief State School Officers. facstaff.wceruw.org/normw/WEBBMonograph6criteria.pdf.

———. 1999. *Alignment of Science and Mathematics Standards and Assessments in Four States*. Research monograph no. 18. Madison, WI: National Institute for Science Education and Washington, DC: Council of Chief State School Officers. facstaff.wceruw.org/normw/WEBBMonograph%2018AlignmentPaper.pdf_Alignment_of_science_and_mathematics_standards_and_assessments_in_four_states.

INDEX

Note: Page locators followed by *f* indicate figures.

T